HSE
Health & Safety
Executive

D0993296

REDUCING NOISE AT WORK

Guidance on the Noise at Work Regulations 1989
L108

HSE BOOKS

This guidance is issued by the Health and Safety Executive.
Following the guidance is not compulsory and you are free to
take other action. But if you do follow the guidance you will
normally be doing enough to comply with the law. Health
and safety inspectors seek to secure compliance with the law
and may refer to this guidance as illustrating good practice.

Contents

(v)

Hearing loss caused by exposure to noise at work continues to be a significant occupational disease. However, it is preventable if:

● manufacturers design machinery to operate more quietly;

● employers introduce workplace policies and controls to reduce exposure to noise; and

● employees make use of the protective measures supplied.

This book is aimed at all those with responsibilities for reducing noise exposure at work. It gives guidance on legal duties, specifically under the Noise at Work Regulations 1989, and offers employers advice on introducing control measures, selecting ear protection, and choosing a competent person to carry out a noise assessment. It also gives advice to the competent person on what is required of a noise assessment.

Each part has a specific audience:

● Part 1 is aimed at employers;

● Part 2 is aimed at designers, manufacturers, importers and suppliers;

● Part 3 is aimed at employers;

● Part 4 is aimed at the 'competent person';

● Part 5 is aimed at employers and engineers;

● Part 6 is aimed at employers.

It is not comprehensive in that it does not repeat guidance already published separately by the Health and Safety Executive (HSE). Relevant publications are listed in the 'References' and 'Further reading' sections. In addition HSE has published guidance on action that should be taken in specific industrial sectors or to deal with noise from particular types of machine. You can obtain up-to-date information on these publications from HSE's InfoLine (see back cover).

This book revises guidance published in 1989 and 1990 by HSE for the Health and Safety Commission (HSC) after widespread consultation with industry (Noise Guides 1-2 ISBN 0 7176 0454 3 and Noise Guides 3-8 ISBN 0 11 885430 5). HSE will continue periodically to review and revise the guidance. If you have any comments on the content or presentation of this book, please write to Health Directorate B5, Health and Safety Executive, Rose Court, 2 Southwark Bridge, London SE1 9HS.

Legal duties of employers to prevent damage to hearing

Introduction

1   Part 1 deals with your legal obligations as an employer to prevent damage to the hearing of workers from excessive noise at work. In addition to the general obligations to safeguard workers' health (including hearing) which you have had since 1975 under the Health and Safety at Work etc Act 1974 (the HSW Act), from 1 January 1990 the law also required you to take specific steps under the Noise at Work Regulations 1989* (the Noise Regulations).

2   The Noise Regulations apply to all workers in Great Britain and to those offshore activities within the scope of the HSW Act except the crews of sea-going ships and aircraft or hovercraft moving under their own power. They are based on a European Community (EC) Directive†requiring similar basic laws throughout the Community on reducing the risk of hearing damage.

3   Employers (and mine or quarry managers) are responsible for action at the workplace, and employees must co-operate with their employer's programme to prevent hearing damage. Machine designers, manufacturers, importers and suppliers also have duties. Guidance on these, and how the HSW Act applies to noisy machinery, is given in Part 2.

General duties under the HSW Act and the Management of Health and Safety at Work Regulations 1992** as amended

4   The Noise Regulations deal only with people at work and with risks to hearing, not other aspects of health, safety and welfare. The duties set out in the HSW Act are more general in scope and mean that you will need to take action if noise causes risks other than hearing damage, or creates risks to people other than workers.[1] Examples of when you might have to take action include:

(a)   if background noise reduces the audibility of a warning sound, you might either have to reduce the noise or solve the problem in some other way, such as providing a louder alarm, or one with a more distinct sound (see International Standard ISO 7731 *Danger signals for workplaces - Auditory danger signals* 1986);

(b)   where people who are not at work are exposed to noise risk by your activities, you will need to do what is reasonably practicable to safeguard their health and safety by action similar to that taken for your employees. Some students in colleges might come into this category, for example those whose courses involve exposure to high levels of noise from machines such as internal combustion engines, turbines and textile machinery, or from other sources such as loud music.

---

* SI 1989/1790 amended by SI 1992/2966 and SI 1996/341; and extended offshore by the Offshore Electricity and Noise Regulations 1997 (SI 1997/1993) which came into force on 21 February 1998.

† Council Directive 86/188/EC of 12 May 1986 on the protection of workers from the risks related to exposure to noise at work.

** SI 1992/2051 amended by SI 1994/2865, SI 1997/135 and SI 1997/1840.

Health surveillance

5   There is a specific requirement under the Management of Health and
Safety at Work Regulations 1992 (the Management Regulations) for you to
provide adequate health surveillance. The Approved Code of Practice to the
Management Regulations[2] sets out the criteria for determining when health
surveillance should be introduced. These criteria are met where there is a
significant risk of hearing loss from exposure to loud noise at work. The
appropriate technique for noise health surveillance is audiometry. HSE has
issued a separate free leaflet on when and how to introduce health surveillance
for exposure to noise.[3]

Citation and commencement

These Regulations may be cited as the Noise at Work Regulations 1989 and shall come into force on 1 January 1990.

Interpretation

(1)   In these Regulations, unless the context otherwise requires -

"daily personal noise exposure" means the level of daily personal noise exposure of an employee ascertained in accordance with Part I of the Schedule to these Regulations, but taking no account of the effect of any personal ear protector used;

"exposed" means exposed whilst at work, and "exposure" shall be construed accordingly;

"the first action level" means a daily personal noise exposure of 85dB(A);

"the peak action level" means a level of peak sound pressure of 200 pascals;

"the second action level" means a daily personal noise exposure of 90dB(A);

(2)   In these Regulations, unless the context otherwise requires, any reference to -

(a)   an employer includes a reference to a self-employed person and any duty imposed by these Regulations on an employer in respect of his employees shall extend to a self-employed person in respect of himself;

(b)   an employee includes a reference to a self-employed person;

and where any duty is placed by these Regulations on an employer in respect of his employees, that employer shall, so far as is reasonably practicable, be under a like duty in respect of any other person at work who may be affected by the work carried on by him.

(3)   Duties under these Regulations imposed upon an employer shall also be imposed upon the manager of a mine or a quarry (within in either case the meaning of section 180 of the Mines and Quarries Act 1954[(a)]) in so far as those duties relate to the mine or quarry or part of the quarry of which he is the manager and to matters under his control.

(4)   Unless the context otherwise requires, any reference in these Regulations to -

(a)   a numbered regulation is a reference to the regulation in these Regulations so numbered; and

(b)   a numbered paragraph is a reference to the paragraph so numbered in the regulation in which the reference appears.

(a)   1954 c.70; section 180 was modified by SI 1974/2013, Schedule 2, Part I, paragraph 3.

Action levels

6   There are three action levels of noise defined in regulation 2:

(a)   the *first action level* - a daily personal noise exposure ($L_{EP,d}$) of 85 dB(A);

(b)   the *second action level* - a daily personal noise exposure ($L_{EP,d}$) of 90 dB(A);

(c)   the *peak action level* - a peak sound pressure of 200 pascals (140 dB re 20 µPa).

7   The formal definition of $L_{EP,d}$ is in the Schedule to the Noise Regulations. It is the daily total personal exposure to noise at work (this figure is normalised to an 8-hour day), taking account of the average levels of noise in working areas and the time spent in them, but taking no account of any ear protectors (earmuffs or earplugs) worn.

8   The peak pressure is the highest pressure reached by the sound wave, for example the peak pressure of the sound impulse generated by a cartridge-operated tool. The peak action level for practical purposes is equivalent to a 'C' weighted peak level of 140 dB(C) (see paragraph 137).

9   The Noise Regulations require you to take certain basic steps where any of your employees is likely to be exposed to noise at or above the first action level. You must also take these steps, together with additional action, where any of your employees is likely to be exposed at or above the second or peak action levels.

10   In practice the action you need to take will usually be determined by the average noise level over the working day from which the value of $L_{EP,d}$ can be calculated. However, where workers are exposed to infrequent but loud impact or explosive noises, eg from guns or cartridge-operated tools, the peak action level may be exceeded even though $L_{EP,d}$ is below the second action level.

The self-employed and homeworkers

11   Regulation 2(2) defines both 'employer' and 'employee' to include self-employed people. So if you are self-employed you will need to take the same action to protect yourself as an employer takes to protect employees, and to use protective equipment on the same basis as employees. Employers will also need to take action to protect those who are employed by them to work at home.

Trainees

12   The Health and Safety (Training for Employment) Regulations 1990[*] require trainees on relevant work training schemes in the workplace (but not those on courses at educational establishments such as universities or schools), to be treated as the employee of the person whose undertaking is providing the training.

Where more than one employer is involved

13   Sometimes your activities may cause employees of other employers to be exposed to noise, for example where contractors take noisy tools into quiet premises to do their job, or they go to do a quiet job in premises that are already noisy. The Noise Regulations place duties on all the employers involved and each will have a responsibility:

[*] SI 1990/1380

(a) to their own employees; and

(b) so far as is reasonably practicable, to anyone else at work who is affected by the work they do (regulation 2(2)).

14   In most cases employers will need to exchange information and collaborate to ensure that they fulfil their duties without unnecessary duplication.

15   On multi-contractor sites or premises, you and the other employers involved will usually need to agree on who is to co-ordinate action to comply with the Noise Regulations. Normally this will be the person in overall control of the work. This person should make sure that responsibilities for measures are clearly defined. For example it will often be appropriate for the employer in overall control to make sure that exposure is assessed and that the information on noise is made available to all affected employers, while the actual employer of each worker provides any training needed. Where contractors and sub-contractors are involved it is usually best for responsibilities to be set out in the contractual arrangements. For construction projects, the principal contractor under the Construction (Design and Management) Regulations 1994[*] should ensure co-operation between all contractors.

16   If you are in charge of premises you should make sure, so far as is reasonably practicable, that visiting workers, including contractors, know where exposure above the action levels is likely, eg ear protection zones, and that they use adequate protection. You may wish to include this information in induction information for new staff and/or in general training.

17   If your employees need to visit noisy premises controlled by someone else (for example, for maintenance or survey work) you will need to consider whether exposure over the action levels is likely, and what can reasonably be done to restrict it (for example by providing ear protection adequate for the worst likely exposure). Employees should co-operate with their employers so far as this is necessary to enable the employers to meet their obligations (see under regulation 10).

[*]SI 1994/3140

Application

(1)   Subject to paragraph (2), these Regulations shall apply -

(a)   in Great Britain; and

(b)   outside Great Britain as sections 1 to 59 and 80 to 82 of the Health and Safety at Work etc. Act 1974 apply by virtue of the provisions of the Health and Safety at Work etc. Act 1974 (Application outside Great Britain) Order 1995.[(a)]

(2)   The duties imposed by these Regulations shall not extend to -

(a)   the master or crew of a sea-going ship or to the employer of such persons, in relation to the normal ship-board activities of a ship's crew under the direction of the master; or

(a) SI 1995/263

(b)   the crew of any aircraft or hovercraft which is moving under its own power or any other person on board any such aircraft or hovercraft who is at work in connection with its operation.

18   The Noise Regulations apply to all work activities in Great Britain and also on offshore installations, wells, pipelines and pipeline works and to certain connected activities within the territorial waters of Great Britain or in designated areas of the UK Continental Shelf. They do not apply to ships at sea or aircraft in flight.

Assessment of exposure

(1)   Every employer shall, when any of his employees is likely to be exposed to the first action level or above or to the peak action level or above, ensure that a competent person makes a noise assessment which is adequate for the purposes -

(a)   of identifying which of his employees are so exposed; and

(b)   of providing him with such information with regard to the noise to which those employees may be exposed as will facilitate compliance with his duties under regulations 7, 8, 9 and 11.

(2)   The noise assessment required by paragraph (1) shall be reviewed when -

(a)   there is reason to suspect that the assessment is no longer valid; or

(b)   there has been a significant change in the work to which the assessment relates;

and, where as a result of the review changes in the assessment are required, those changes shall be made.

Purpose of the noise assessment

19   Your noise assessment will identify the daily noise exposure of all your employees who might be at risk of hearing damage, and will give you information to help you decide what you will do to control the noise exposure. It will enable you to draw up an informed action plan to reduce the risk of hearing damage. Your noise assessment is not a one-off activity - you will need to arrange for it to be kept up to date and amend your action plan accordingly.

Five steps to noise assessment

20   You will need to take five basic steps in assessing the risks from noise in the workplace:

Step 1   Look to see whether there is likely to be a noise hazard (see paragraphs 21-23).

Step 2   Identify all workers likely to be exposed to the hazard (see paragraphs 24-25).

Step 3   Evaluate the risks arising from the hazard - establish the noise exposures to help you decide what further action is appropriate to comply with regulations 7, 8, 9 and 11 (see paragraphs 26-31 and Part 4).

Step 4 Record the findings (see regulation 5 and paragraphs 37-40).

Step 5 Review the assessment and revise it if necessary (see paragraphs 33-35).

Note: Steps 3 and 5 must be undertaken by a competent person (see paragraph 36 and Part 3). You may wish to ask the competent person also to undertake Step 4.

Step 1 - Deciding whether a noise assessment is needed

21   You are required under the Management Regulations to make an assessment of risks to health and safety in the workplace. This risk assessment will enable you to come to a preliminary decision on whether there is likely to be a hazard from noise and therefore whether a specific noise assessment is needed under regulation 4(1). You can usually reach this decision without making detailed noise measurements.

22   As a rough guide, noise is likely to be at hazardous levels wherever people have to shout or have difficulty being heard clearly by someone about 2 m away. Where there is any doubt you should arrange for some measurements of the noise to be taken in a few representative places. If this suggests that any workers might be exposed to the first action level or above you will need to carry out a full noise assessment.

23   It is always likely that the peak action level might be exceeded where workers are exposed to loud noises from explosive sources, such as cartridge-operated tools or detonators, or where there are high levels of impact noise.

Step 2 - Who might be exposed?

24   In identifying the noise hazard, you will need to consider all people at work who might be exposed, including contractors, people who share the workplace, maintenance personnel, visitors etc. You will also need to consider the exposure of your own employees when working away from the main site including any home workers. Paragraphs 13-17 give guidance on co-operation with other employers whose employees may be exposed to noise from your process or at whose premises your own employees work.

New and expectant mothers and young people

25   The Management Regulations (as amended) require you to take particular account of risks to new and expectant mothers when assessing risks from noise. HSE has issued separate guidance on protecting pregnant workers' health at work.[4] The Management Regulations (as amended) also prohibit you from employing young people under 18 years old where there is a risk to health from noise. HSE has produced guidance which gives information on the particular risks to young people you should consider in your risk assessment, including noise.[5] There is no evidence that young workers face greater risk of damaged hearing from exposure to noise than other workers. Compliance with the Noise Regulations should protect their hearing.

Step 3 - Noise assessments

26   Once you have identified that there is a likely noise hazard, you will need to assess the risks to the workers exposed. Only by doing this will you be able to determine what action you will need to take to control the hazard. The noise assessment will give you information about your employees' exposure to noise and advise you what you can do to reduce it. This means you will need to arrange for a competent person to carry out a noise assessment (advice on

choosing a competent person is given in Part 3), and obtain reliable information about work patterns and the noise sources. In planning this it is important that you consult the affected employees and their safety or employee representatives; this will help ensure their co-operation with any control measures that might be needed.

27   The competent person can often make an adequate assessment without making a detailed measurement of every individual worker's exposure. For example:

(a)   where groups of workers regularly perform similar tasks, sample measurements on a group or activity basis might be adequate provided that the noise exposure is representative of individuals within the group;

(b)   where groups of workers are regularly employed in an area throughout which the noise level is reasonably uniform, you might base the assessment on noise levels measured in the working area and the length of time that workers are likely to spend there.

28   Some workers are exposed to noise levels which vary considerably either during the day or from one day to another, for example because they visit a number of noisy areas, or because they do a variety of jobs requiring intermittent use of noisy tools and machines. In these cases no single day or other period of time can be considered to be representative of their noise exposure. So sometimes it will be impracticable or of little use to make an accurate measurement of $L_{EP,d}$ for these workers. In these circumstances the most practical course will usually be to treat all working areas where the average noise level, or 'equivalent continuous sound level' (A-weighted L_{eq}) is 85 or 90 dB(A) or more as places where the corresponding action levels are likely to be exceeded (see also paragraph 48).

29   Detailed advice on how to carry out a noise assessment is given in Part 4.

Deciding what further action needs to be taken

30   The noise assessment should have identified who at work will be exposed at or above the various action levels and where and in what circumstances that will occur. This will enable you to decide in general terms what action you will have to take under regulations 7, 8, 9 and 11 to reduce noise exposure, provide information and set up ear protection zones. However, you will often require further information, for example on the best way of reducing noise by engineering means, and you might need to supplement your noise assessment with more detailed studies. The assessment will only be adequate, and so comply with regulation 4(1)(b), if it provides enough information to enable you to take the most appropriate action - guidance on this is given in the paragraphs following regulations 7, 8, 9 and 11.

Implementing the noise assessment results

31   It is for you to determine how far to seek the advice of the competent person on following up the noise assessment. You might wish to ask the competent person to assess current controls and to make recommendations for further action. But it is your responsibility to ensure that the information obtained in the noise assessment is translated into effective action to reduce noise exposure, and you may wish to take broader considerations into account in deciding what you need to do. It is often useful to draw up an action plan setting out priorities and targets in collaboration with the employees concerned and their representatives.

Step 4 - Record the findings

32   Detailed advice is given in paragraphs 37-40 following regulation 5.

Step 5 - Review of noise assessments

33   You will need to keep the noise assessment up to date. After you have made your initial decision on the action required under the Noise Regulations, you will need to continue to collect information to keep the noise control and personal protection programmes under review. You should review the assessment whenever there are any significant changes in the work or the equipment used, or any other reason to suppose it is no longer valid. Also, you may be able to make a more complete noise assessment at a later date where circumstances change, ie where earlier practical difficulties which limited the information collected (eg as described in paragraph 28) are removed or where improved equipment and assessment procedures become available.

34   Changes that might create the need for a review include:

(a)   installation or removal of machinery;

(b)   substantial changes in workload, work pattern and exposure time, processed materials, processes or machine speeds;

(c)   changes in building structure or machine layout;

(d)   machine wear or general deterioration;

(e)   modifications to machinery and introduction of automation;

(f)   the introduction of a noise control or hearing conservation programme.

35   Even where there have been no obvious changes, you should not leave workplaces for long periods without checking whether there is a need for a review, for example because of gradual changes in noise levels due to machine wear, the introduction of new technology or changes in work practices. You can make spot checks by establishing a few selected locations where you can periodically measure the sound pressure level, for example places where exposure is high or a gradual increase in noise levels is likely. The interval between checks will depend on local circumstances but, for most kinds of machinery, the maximum would be about two years.

Competent persons

36   You have to make sure that the noise assessment is done by a competent person, that is someone able to produce an assessment which complies with regulation 4(1). The competent person will not necessarily have to make all noise measurements personally; often he or she will be able to supervise the collection of information on levels of noise and exposure, and its use in the final assessment. Advice on the skills and knowledge needed by a competent person, and their selection and training is given in Part 3.

Assessment records

Following any noise assessment made pursuant to regulation 4(1), the employer shall ensure that an adequate record of that assessment, and of any review thereof carried out pursuant to regulation 4(2), is kept until a further noise assessment is made pursuant to regulation 4(1).

Recording of exposure

37   The best person to complete the noise assessment record is the competent person. An adequate record would normally include details of:

(a)   the workplaces, areas, jobs or people assessed;

(b)   measurement locations and durations and any noise control measures being used at the time;

(c)   the work patterns and calculations of daily exposure;

(d)   daily personal noise exposures $L_{EP,d}$ where they are above the first action level;

(e)   peak noise exposure levels where they are above the peak action level;

(f)   the sources of noise;

(g)   any further information necessary to help compliance with the reduction of noise exposure;

(h)   the date of the assessment;

(i)   who made the assessment.

38   Additional information that you might incorporate in the record includes:

(a)   details of the instruments used, the sensitivity calibration checks and the last periodic verification;

(b)   a tabular record of the noise exposure resulting from various tasks or activities, identified by person, work area or operation;

(c)   a plan showing levels of noise at various places in the premises and a record of who works there and typical working times;

(d)   a record of the type of workplace likely to be visited by employees who move about and the associated levels of noise and exposures;

(e)   recommended actions for reducing noise exposure.

39   You may keep the record in any readily retrievable and easily understood form. No single form will be suitable for all circumstances. Examples of some suggested record forms designed for particular purposes are shown in Part 4.

40   You must make sure a record of the assessment is kept until a new one is made. However, it will usually be useful to keep records longer than this to provide information on long-term trends, even though this is not required by the Noise Regulations.

Reduction of risk of hearing damage

Every employer shall reduce the risk of damage to the hearing of his employees from exposure to noise to the lowest level reasonably practicable.

General reduction of risk of hearing damage

41   There is a quantifiable risk of hearing damage from exposures between 85 dB(A) (first action level) and 90 dB(A) (second action level), and a residual though small risk below 85 dB(A). This means that, in addition to taking the steps required by the Noise Regulations to reduce exposure below the second action level, you will need to consider whether more can be done to control noise exposures to further reduce any risk to hearing. As an example, a positive purchasing policy (see paragraph 49) should eventually bring real benefit.

Reduction of noise exposure

Every employer shall, when any of his employees is likely to be exposed to the second action level or above or to the peak action level or above, reduce, so far as is reasonably practicable (other than by the provision of personal ear protectors), the exposure to noise of that employee.

Programme of measures

42   Where employees are exposed at or above the second or peak action levels you will have to reduce exposure as far as reasonably practicable by means other than provision of personal ear protectors. To achieve this you will need to implement a programme of control measures. Where adequate reduction is not reasonably practicable in the short term, the programme should continue to operate as long as necessary, and should include regular reviews of the feasibility of further noise reduction, taking account of developments in noise control techniques. Detailed advice is given in Part 5.

43   The most reliable way of limiting exposure is to reduce the level of workplace noise. You should already, as part of the noise assessment, have identified the sources of noise in the workplace and ways in which the noise levels can be reduced. You now need to plan a programme of action. This means:

(a)   identifying which steps are reasonably practicable to reduce the noise level by engineering means;

(b)   establishing priorities for action;

(c)   ensuring that action is taken;

(d)   reassessing noise exposure.

44   In establishing priorities, your aim should be to identify where action will bring most benefit. Factors to take into account are:

(a)   the number of people who would benefit from the noise reduction measures;

(b)   the noise exposure levels involved;

(c)   the cost of any changes to reduce noise exposure and how practical they will be to introduce. In general higher priority should be given to the more cost-effective measures;

(d)   how effective any controls will be;

(e)   any factors which make reliance on personal ear protection especially undesirable, such as strenuous work in a hot, dirty environment.

45   Programmes to control noise by engineering means will only be effective if the staff working on them are competent in noise control engineering, or are advised by someone who is. Sometimes, however, the noise can be reduced by more fundamental changes, such as using a different, quieter process, and here knowledge of the process and alternative ways of doing the job may be more important.

46   There are many ways of reducing noise and no single technique will be appropriate for every situation. Some of the measures that should be considered are outlined in Part 5. HSE has also published *Sound solutions*, a book of useful case studies outlining noise reduction techniques used by different industries.[6] A programme of engineering noise control should adopt a systematic approach to identifying, designing and introducing the right measures, an assessment after installation, and further action if needed to overcome any unforeseen practical difficulties that may arise.

47   Limiting the time spent in noisy areas can also help to restrict daily personal noise exposure but usually only to a limited extent - halving the exposure time will reduce $L_{EP,d}$ by only 3 dB(A). Also, if you have to rely on controlling exposure time to reduce noise exposure, you must control it effectively. Any opportunity to provide short periods of relief from noise, such as in a noise refuge, will help by allowing some recuperation and preventing the need to wear ear protection continuously, even if this does not significantly reduce $L_{EP,d}$.

Workers with variable exposure to noise

48   Where noise exposure is highly variable, either from day to day or job to job or from the use of mobile tools and machinery (for example in some farm work or in premises where workers must move about a great deal) you might find it difficult to identify how far it is reasonably practicable to reduce exposure. However, your noise assessment should have identified the main sources of noise exposure, and appropriate measures might then include:

(a)   replacing noisy equipment or tools with quieter ones, perhaps phased in over time;

(b)   making special arrangements to limit noise exposure, particularly if the noisy area visited is not usually occupied, for example by arranging for repairs in a normally unattended machine room to be done when other noisy machinery is shut down.

Selecting machinery

49   Noise reduction programmes are only likely to be effective if they include a positive purchasing policy which makes sure you take noise into account when selecting machinery. When making enquiries, you should ask potential suppliers for information on the noise emission of machines and whether they are likely to cause exposure at or above the first or peak action level (which suppliers are required by regulation 12 to provide*). HSE has published a free leaflet *Keep the noise down*, giving advice to purchasers of workplace machinery.[7]

---

* Regulation 12 modifies the duties manufacturers, suppliers etc already have under section 6 of the HSW Act to include provision of information on the noise likely to be generated. Their duties to deal with noise emission of the machinery they supply are outlined in Part 2 which also describes ways in which information is likely to be supplied.

50   Data provided by suppliers will usually be the results of tests made under standardised conditions of installation and load. You should use this data when comparing different machines, before deciding which to buy, and to predict whether you will need to do a noise assessment when you bring the machines into use.

51   As an alternative to relying on standard test data, you may wish to make arrangements with the supplier for machines to be delivered with a guarantee that the noise after installation will not exceed an agreed value. If you do this you should check the noise emission when you bring the machine into use.

52   Where you find it is necessary to purchase machinery which causes workers to be exposed over the action levels, you will find that keeping a record of the reasons for the decision will help guide future action, for example by providing those responsible for future machine specifications with information on improvements that are needed.

Ear protection

(1)   Every employer shall ensure, so far as is practicable, that when any of his employees is likely to be exposed to the first action level or above in circumstances where the daily personal noise exposure of that employee is likely to be less than 90 dB(A), that employee is provided, at his request, with suitable and efficient personal ear protectors.

(2)   Every employer shall ensure, so far as is practicable, that when any of his employees is likely to be exposed to the second action level or above or to the peak action level or above, that employee is provided with suitable personal ear protectors which, when properly worn, can reasonably be expected to keep the risk of damage to that employee's hearing to below that arising from exposure to the second action level or, as the case may be, to the peak action level.

(3)   Any personal ear protectors provided by virtue of this regulation shall comply with any enactment (whether in an Act or an instrument) which implements in Great Britain any provision on design or manufacture with respect to health and safety in any relevant Community Directive listed in Schedule 1 to the Personal Protective Equipment at Work Regulations 1992[(a)] which is applicable to those ear protectors.

(a) SI 1992/2966

The need for ear protectors

53   The duty to provide ear protectors depends on the exposure level:

Between the first and second action levels

Where employees are exposed between the first and second action levels you have to provide protectors to employees who ask for them but the Noise Regulations do not make it compulsory for workers to use them.

At or above the second and peak action levels

You have to provide ear protectors to all workers likely to be exposed at or above the second or peak action levels. Under regulation 10 you have to ensure the ear protectors are used, and your employees are required to use them. Under regulation 11 you will need to provide information about the protectors and how to obtain them.

Choosing a suitable type of protector

54   Detailed advice on types of protector and their selection is given in Part 6.

Regulation 9

Ear protection zones

(1)   Every employer shall, in respect of any premises under his control, ensure, so far as is reasonably practicable, that -

(a)   each ear protection zone is demarcated and identified by means of the sign specified for the purpose of indicating "ear protection must be worn" in paragraph 3.3 of Part II of Schedule 1 to the Health and Safety (Safety Signs and Signals) Regulations 1996[(a)] and which sign shall include such text as indicates -

(i)   that it is an ear protection zone, and

(ii)   the need for his employees to wear personal ear protectors whilst in any such zone; and

(b)   none of his employees enters any such zone unless that employee is wearing personal ear protectors.

(2)   In this regulation, "ear protection zone" means any part of the premises referred to in paragraph (1) where any employee is likely to be exposed to the second action level or above or to the peak action level or above.

(a) SI 1996/341

Ear protection zones

55   Your noise assessment should have identified those areas of your premises where any of your employees are likely to be exposed at or above the second or peak action levels. So far as is reasonably practicable you will have to identify these areas as 'ear protection zones' and ensure that employees who enter any such areas are wearing ear protectors.

56   Wherever reasonably practicable you will need to mark ear protection zones with signs showing that they are areas where ear protectors are needed (see Figure 1). You should locate these signs at all entrances to the zones, and at appropriate places within the zones as necessary.

57   Where it is not reasonably practicable to mark ear protection zones, for example where the work requires people to move the noise sources about a great deal, you should make adequate alternative arrangements to help make sure that employees know where or when protectors should be worn. These could include:

(a)   attaching signs to tools warning that users of them must wear ear protectors;

(b)   written and oral instructions on how to recognise where and when protectors should be worn, for example by designating particular tasks or operations as ones where protectors must be used.

EAR PROTECTION ZONE

EAR PROTECTORS MUST BE WORN

Figure 1 Example of pictogram indicating ear protectors must be worn (white on a circular blue background)

(From the Health and Safety (Safety Signs and Signals) Regulations 1996.)

Regulation 10

Maintenance and use of equipment

(1)   Every employer shall -

(a)   ensure, so far as is practicable, that anything provided by him to or for the benefit of an employee in compliance with his duties under these Regulations (other than personal ear protectors provided pursuant to regulation 8(1)) is fully and properly used; and

(b)   ensure, so far as is practicable, that anything provided by him in compliance with his duties under these Regulations is maintained in an efficient state, in efficient working order and in good repair.

(2)   Every employee shall, so far as is practicable, fully and properly use personal ear protectors when they are provided by his employer pursuant to regulation 8(2) and any other protective measures provided by his employer in compliance with his duties under these Regulations; and, if the employee discovers any defect therein, he shall report it forthwith to his employer.

Noise control equipment

58   You need to ensure, so far as is practicable, that anything you provide under the Noise Regulations (except for ear protectors where exposure is between the first and second action levels) is properly used and that all equipment is maintained. This means that you will need to carry out regular checks and introduce a system for reporting any defects or problems to someone with authority and responsibility for remedial action. You will need to put right any deficiencies promptly.

59   You should introduce a planned programme of maintenance including:

(a)   inspecting the noise control equipment (such as silencers or enclosures) periodically to make sure it is kept in good condition;

(b)   monitoring the equipment's effectiveness. Spot checks of the noise level at pre-selected locations will usually be adequate (see also paragraph 35);

(c)   reporting the results of these checks to someone with responsibility and authority for taking remedial action.

Ear protectors

60   People are often reluctant to use ear protectors, and even where they start to use them they can easily get out of the habit. You therefore need to introduce a systematic programme to maintain use, taking into account the following elements:

(a)   the firm's *safety policy*. This should include a strong commitment on personal protection;

(b)   *signs and warning notices* to ensure awareness of where and when protectors should be used (see under regulation 11);

(c)   *clear responsibilities*. You should identify who is responsible for the ear protection programme and the distribution and maintenance of protectors;

(d)   *information, instruction and training* for all employees on the risks and the action they should take (see under regulation 11);

(e)   *records*. These should include details of the issue of ear protectors, arrangements for ensuring users know where and how to use them, and any problems people encounter in their use;

(f)   *monitoring* including spot checks to find out whether the ear protectors are being used. You should keep a record and introduce a system to enable people to report deficiencies to a person with responsibility and authority for remedial action. Where an employee is not using ear protection properly you should ask them why, and either resolve the difficulty or give and record a verbal warning. Where people persistently fail to use protectors properly you should give them a written warning and follow normal disciplinary procedures.

61   You will need to arrange for someone to inspect reusable ear protectors periodically and to repair or replace them if necessary. If your employees use disposable protectors, you should check that supplies are continuously available, and fill dispensers up regularly. You should introduce a system for employees to report any damaged, defective or lost protectors.

62   You should make proper provision for storage of reusable protectors, such as:

(a)   storage bags for earmuffs;

(b)   clean lockers where employees can keep them with other clothing; and

(c)   strong cases for earplugs.

63   You should also ensure that any special cleaning materials needed for hygiene are available to users.

Employees' duties

64   Programmes for controlling noise exposure are most likely to succeed when there is co-operation between yourself and your employees. The involvement of safety representatives and other employee representatives will be invaluable in promoting this co-operation. Employees have a duty to comply with and use the measures you provide under the Noise Regulations, and this will include:

(a)   using noise control measures, such as exhaust silencers and machine enclosures, in accordance with your instructions;

(b)   wearing ear protection in accordance with instructions provided at or above the second or peak action levels and at all times in areas marked as ear protection zones. It is in their own interest to use protectors made available for exposures between the first and second action levels, though this is not a statutory duty under the Regulations;

(c)   taking care of ear protectors and noise control equipment they need to use;

(d)   reporting, in accordance with your procedures, any defect found in the ear protectors or other protective measures or any difficulties in using them.

65   In addition, under the HSW Act, employees are required generally to co-operate with their employer to enable the employer to carry out legal duties.

Provision of information to employees

Every employer shall, in respect of any premises under his control, provide each of his employees who is likely to be exposed to the first action level or above or to the peak action level or above with adequate information, instruction and training on -

(a)   the risk of damage to that employee's hearing that such exposure may cause;

(b)   what steps that employee can take to minimise that risk;

(c)   the steps that that employee must take in order to obtain the personal ear protectors referred to in regulation 8(1); and

(d)   that employee's obligations under these Regulations.

Information, instruction and training for employees

66   Where employees are likely to be exposed at or above any of the action levels you are required to provide information, instruction and training including:

(a)   the likely noise exposure and the risk to hearing the noise creates;

(b)   where and how people can obtain ear protectors;

(c)   how to report defects in ear protectors and noise control equipment;

(d) the employee's duties under the Noise Regulations;

(e) what the employee should do to minimise the risk, such as the proper way to use ear protectors and other equipment, how to look after them, and where to use ear protectors.

67   You should also advise employees that if any symptoms appear, such as difficulty in understanding speech in conversation or when using the telephone, or permanent ringing in the ears (tinnitus) it is in their own interest to seek medical advice.

68   Health and safety staff and managers can provide information, instruction and training in different ways, including:

(a) oral explanations;

(b) individual counselling and training;

(c) leaflets and posters;

(d) films, videotapes and sound recordings;

(e) short local training sessions.

69   No single way will be suitable for all circumstances, and you will need to reinforce the messages from time to time. You should draw the employee's attention to any relevant advice published by HSE or HSC.

70   You should make sure that you give information in a way which the employee can be expected to understand (for example you might need to make special arrangements if the employee does not understand English or cannot read).

Employee representatives and safety representatives

71   Working with trade union-appointed safety representatives or other employee representatives can be a very useful means of communicating on health and safety matters in your workplace. You are required by the Safety Representatives and Safety Committees Regulations 1977[*] and the Offshore Installations (Safety Representatives and Safety Committees) Regulations 1989[†] to make certain information available to safety representatives appointed under the Regulations. The representatives are entitled to inspect some of your documents which will normally include records of noise assessments covering the employees represented. You should make sure the representatives know how the information can be obtained and give them any necessary explanations of their meaning. There is also a duty on employers to provide information to employee representatives elected under the Health and Safety (Consultation with Employees) Regulations 1996,[**] which apply to groups of workers who are not covered by a trade union-appointed safety representative.

---

[*] SI 1977/500. The Regulations, an associated Approved Code of Practice and Guidance Notes are published in a Health and Safety Commission booklet *Safety representatives and safety committees* L87 (HSE Books 1996 ISBN 0 7176 1220 1)

[†] SI 1989/971

[**] SI 1996/1513 and explained in *A guide to the Health and Safety (Consultation with Employees) Regulations 1996* L95 (HSE Books 1996 ISBN 0 7176 1234 1)

Modification of duties of manufacturers etc. of articles for use at work and articles of fairground equipment

In the case of articles for use at work or articles of fairground equipment, section 6 of the Health and Safety at Work etc. Act 1974[a] (which imposes general duties on manufacturers etc. as regards articles for use at work, substances and articles of fairground equipment) shall be modified so that any duty imposed on any person by subsection (1) of that section shall include a duty to ensure that, where any such article as is referred to therein is likely to cause any employee to be exposed to the first action level or above or to the peak action level or above, adequate information is provided concerning the noise likely to be generated by that article.

(a) 1974 c.37; Section 6 was amended by the Consumer Protection Act 1987 (c.43), Schedule 3, paragraph 1.

The need to provide information on noise

72   If a machine is likely to cause people at work to receive a daily personal noise exposure at or above the first action level or peak action level, regulation 12 places a duty on the manufacturer, designer, importer and supplier to ensure that adequate information is provided on the noise likely to be generated. You can find further information on regulation 12 in Part 2, which also offers guidance on relevant requirements of the Supply of Machinery (Safety) Regulations 1992 (as amended in 1994).[*]

[*] SI 1992/ 3073 amended by SI 1994/2063

Exemptions

(1)   Subject to paragraph (2), the Health and Safety Executive may, by a certificate in writing, exempt any employer from -

(a)   the requirement in regulation 7, where the daily personal noise exposure of the relevant employee, averaged over a week and ascertained in accordance with Part II of the Schedule to these Regulations, is below 90 dB(A) and there are adequate arrangements for ensuring that that average will not be exceeded; or

(b)   the requirement in regulation 8(2), where -

(i)   the daily personal noise exposure of the relevant employee, averaged over a week and ascertained in accordance with Part II of the Schedule to these Regulations, is below 90 dB(A) and there are adequate arrangements for ensuring that that average will not be exceeded,

(ii)   the full and proper use of the personal ear protectors referred to in that paragraph would be likely to cause risks to the health or safety of the user, or

(iii)   (subject to the use of personal ear protectors affording the highest degree of personal protection which it is reasonably practicable to achieve in the circumstances) compliance with that requirement is not reasonably practicable;

and any such exemption may be granted subject to conditions and to a limit of time and may be revoked at any time by a certificate in writing.

(2)   The Executive shall not grant any such exemption unless, having regard to the circumstances of the case and in particular to -

(a)   the conditions, if any, which it proposes to attach to the exemption; and

(b)   any other requirements imposed by or under any enactments which apply to the case,

it is satisfied that the health and safety of persons who are likely to be affected by the exemption will not be prejudiced in consequence of it.

Powers of HSE to grant exemptions from regulation 7 and/or regulation 8(2)

73   HSE may grant exemptions from specific requirements of the Noise Regulations provided they are satisfied that the health and safety of people who are likely to be affected by the exemption will not be prejudiced as a result. HSE may grant exemptions subject to time limitation and conditions, and may revoke exemptions. If they are to grant an exemption, HSE will normally require you to agree with them a programme to make sure you control and check noise exposure, and introduce improvements as soon as reasonably practicable.

74   HSE may only consider exemptions where:

(a)   there are substantial fluctuations in noise exposure from day to day and you can exercise effective control better by averaging exposure over a week;

(b)   the compulsory use of ear protectors might increase danger overall, outweighing the risk of hearing damage; or

(c)   it is not practicable to use ear protectors meeting the requirements of regulation 8(2), provided people wear the most appropriate ear protection.

Applications for exemptions

What you need to do to apply for an exemption

75   You should make any application for exemption to the authority responsible for enforcing health and safety legislation in your premises. If in doubt about who this is, consult your HSE local office. There is no standard form, but you will need to supply full supporting information prepared by someone with a good understanding of the problem and ways of combating it, including:

(a)   details of the work activity, with as much information about the noise characteristics as possible, including sound pressure levels, the octave-band spectra and time history, and a statement of typical daily exposure periods of the employees affected;

(b)   the justification for the application;

(c)   what you are currently doing or propose to do about reducing the risk of hearing damage to the lowest level reasonably practicable (regulation 6);

(d)   how you propose to check noise exposure and the effectiveness of control measures;

(e) details of your discussions with the workers affected and/or their safety representatives, and what information you have given them about risks;

(f) how you propose to review the need for the exemption and incorporate improvements as soon as reasonably practicable.

76 If you are seeking exemption under regulation 13(1)(a) or (b)(i), ie from the need to average noise exposure over 8 hours, you will need to provide additional information on:

(a) how you propose to limit the weekly average (eg what the working arrangements will be);

(b) your monitoring system for checking exposures over the week.

77 You should base your information on the worst likely situation.

78 If you are seeking exemption under regulation 13(1)(b)(ii), ie from using ear protectors because of a greater health and safety risk, you will need to provide additional information on:

(a) the source of the noise that makes ear protectors necessary;

(b) what the risk is if your employees use ear protectors;

(c) what you are currently doing to protect against that risk;

(d) the existing arrangements for identifying individuals who might have particular difficulty in hearing warning sounds (eg because of hearing loss) and for ensuring their safety;

(e) how possible it is to reduce noise exposures in the short term and through a planned long-term noise reduction programme;

(f) how possible it is to provide alternative safety arrangements (eg for warning employees or reducing the risk).

79 If you are seeking exemption under regulation 13(1)(b)(iii), ie that ear protectors cannot provide the required degree of protection, you will need to provide additional information on:

(a) what type of ear protectors or combination of ear protection you will use to ensure the highest protection reasonably practicable;

(b) how possible it is to reduce exposure by other means including noise reduction and reducing the time employees spend in noisy areas.

How HSE will deal with your application for an exemption

80 HSE will acknowledge your application promptly (within HSE Citizen's Charter targets) and give you the opportunity of an exchange of views on your application if you want it. The final decision on your application will be given in writing. Information on how to complain if you are unhappy with the way we have dealt with you is included in a free HSE booklet.[8]

Revocations

81 If HSE intends to vary any conditions in or revoke an exemption, usually after an exchange of views, you will be informed in writing.

Modifications relating to the Ministry of Defence etc

(1)   In this regulation, any reference to -

(a)   "visiting forces" is a reference to visiting forces within the meaning of any provision of Part I of the Visiting Forces Act 1952[a]; and

(b)   "headquarters or organisation" is a reference to a headquarters or organisation designated for the purposes of the International Headquarters and Defence Organisations Act 1964[b].

(2)   The Secretary of State for Defence may, in the interests of national security, by a certificate in writing exempt -

(a)   Her Majesty's Forces;

(b)   visiting forces; or

(c)   any member of a visiting force working in or attached to any headquarters or organisation,

from any requirement imposed by these Regulations and any such exemption may be granted subject to conditions and to a limit of time and may be revoked at any time by a certificate in writing, except that, before any such exemption is granted, the Secretary of State for Defence must be satisfied that suitable arrangements have been made for the assessment of the health risks created by the work involving exposure to noise and for adequately controlling the exposure to noise of persons to whom the exemption relates.

(a) 1952 c.67.

(b) 1964 c.5.

Revocation

Regulation 44 of the Woodworking Machines Regulations 1974[a] is hereby revoked.

(a) SI 1974/903 to which there are amendments not relevant to these Regulations.

Part I

Daily personal noise exposure of employees

The daily personal noise exposure of an employee ($L_{EP,d}$) is expressed in dB(A) and is ascertained using the formula:

$$L_{EP,d} = 10 \log_{10} \left\{ \frac{1}{T_0} \int_0^{T_e} \left[\frac{p_A(t)}{p_0} \right]^2 dt \right\}$$

where -

T_e = the duration of the person's personal exposure to sound;

T_0 = 8 hours = 28,800 seconds;

p_0 = 20 μPa; and

$P_A(t)$ = the time-varying value of A-weighted instantaneous sound pressure in pascals in the undisturbed field in air at atmospheric pressure to which the person is exposed (in the locations occupied during the day), or the pressure of the disturbed field adjacent to the person's head adjusted to provide a notional equivalent undisturbed field pressure.

Part II

Weekly average of daily personal noise exposure of employees

The weekly average of an employee's daily personal noise exposure ($L_{EP,w}$) is expressed in dB(A) and is ascertained using the formula:

$$L_{EP,w} = 10 \log_{10} \left[\frac{1}{5} \sum_{k=1}^{k=m} 10^{\,0.1(L_{EP,d})_k} \right]$$

where -

$(L_{EP,d})_k$ = the values of $L_{EP,d}$ for each of the m working days in the week being considered.

82   The weekly average daily personal noise exposure is for use for applications for exemptions only.

Duties of designers, manufacturers, importers and suppliers

Overview

- What are my legal duties in relation to manufacturing and supplying noisy machinery?

- When do I need to provide information to the buyer?

- What information should I provide?

- What are the limitations of the information?

- What test procedures should be used?

Introduction

83   Part 2 reviews the legal obligations of designers, manufacturers, importers and suppliers of plant and machinery for use at work to provide noise information and to control noise emissions from machinery.

Summary of legal duties

84   Section 6 of the Health and Safety at Work etc Act 1974 (the HSW Act) imposes general duties on designers, manufacturers, importers and suppliers to design and construct articles for use at work that are safe and without risks to health and to provide information needed for their safe use.

85   Regulation 12 of the Noise at Work Regulations 1989 (the Noise Regulations) modifies section 6 of the HSW Act specifically to require designers, manufacturers, importers and suppliers to provide adequate information on the noise likely to be generated if the use of their product is likely to expose employees at or above the first (85 dB(A)) or peak (200 pascals) action levels.

86   The Supply of Machinery (Safety) Regulations 1992 (the SM(S) Regulations) (as amended in 1994) require manufacturers, importers and suppliers of noisy machinery to:

- design and construct such machinery so that the risks from noise emissions are reduced to the lowest level taking account of technical progress (Schedule 3 section 1.5.8);

- provide information on noise emissions which reach or exceed specified levels in the information/instructions accompanying machines (Schedule 3 section 1.7.4).

87   General guidance on all the requirements of the SM(S) Regulations is available from the Department of Trade and Industry.[9]

88   There are a few other statutory provisions which set noise limits in specific cases. In particular, noise requirements for some machinery used outdoors are incorporated in the Construction Plant and Equipment (Harmonisation of Noise Emission Standards) Regulations 1985 and 1988 which implement a range of European Community Directives. There is currently under negotiation a proposal for a Directive on noise emissions from equipment used outdoors (COM (1998) 46 Final) which will consolidate and add to the existing Directives and will in due course need to be implemented through UK Regulations.

Section 6 of the HSW Act as amended by regulation 12 of the Noise Regulations

89   To comply with their duties under this legislation, designers, manufacturers, importers and suppliers of machinery and equipment for use at work will need to ensure, so far as is reasonably practicable, that the machinery and equipment is safe and without risks to health at all times when it is being set, used, cleaned or maintained by a person at work. This means that designers etc should aim at least to reduce the sound pressure levels likely to be generated under all reasonably foreseeable use so that people at work are not exposed above the first or peak action level. All relevant research, testing and examination should be carried out to ensure this.

90   Where such noise reduction is not reasonably practicable, information on the level of noise emission and usage must be provided with the machinery and equipment and should be reviewed if serious risks to health or safety are identified. Also, people who erect or install articles for use at work must ensure, so far as reasonably practicable, that they do not create risks to health or safety when they are subsequently used.

When information should be provided

91   Machine suppliers may not know the exact noise exposure their products will cause in use. They will therefore need to make an assessment, taking into account all reasonably foreseeable ways in which the machine might be used, to decide whether it is likely to cause exposure over the

action levels in paragraph 85. For example, when deciding whether noise information is needed for a plastics granulator, the kinds and hardness of the plastics it is capable of processing need to be taken into account. Similarly, the maker of a textile machine, commonly used in an array with other similar machines, will need to assume there will be some increase in noise level over that from a single machine tested in isolation.

92   In practice, compliance with the more specific requirements of the SM(S) Regulations (see paragraphs 93-106) is likely to ensure compliance with regulation 6 of the HSW Act and regulation 12 of the Noise Regulations. However, the SM(S) Regulations do not apply to machinery first supplied or put into service in the European Community before 1993. Suppliers of second-hand machinery may be able to rely on information originally supplied with the machine if this is available. However, they may need to provide new information if, for example, the original information is no longer available or the machine has been significantly modified, so that the existing information is no longer valid.

Supply of Machinery (Safety) Regulations 1992 (as amended in 1994)

Reduction of noise emissions

93   Schedule 3 section 1.5.8 of the SM(S) Regulations requires manufacturers, importers and suppliers of noisy machinery to design and construct such machinery so that the risks from noise emissions are reduced to the lowest level taking account of technical progress. This will involve an engineering appraisal of the feasibility of noise control and the application of effective techniques by engineers familiar with noise control methods.

Information on noise that should be provided

94   Schedule 3 section 1.7.4 of the SM(S) Regulations requires that information on noise emissions which reach specified levels must be provided in instructions accompanying machines. The purpose of the information is:

- to alert purchasers to the noise emission of machines, and help them in selecting suitable products and designing the layout of areas where they will be used; and

- to enable them to plan their arrangements to protect their workers.

95   The principal information which must be supplied is:

- if the sound pressure level does not exceed 70 dB(A) then this should be indicated;

- if the equivalent continuous A-weighted sound pressure level at workstations is at or above 70 dB(A) the level should be given;

- the peak C-weighted instantaneous sound pressure level, where this exceeds 63 Pa (130 dB) in relation to 20 μPa;

- the sound power level emitted by the machinery, where the equivalent continuous A-weighted sound pressure level at workstations exceeds 85 dB(A) (in the case of very large machinery only the sound pressure level around the machine need be indicated);

- any measures needed to keep noise under control when the machine is used. For example, if a machine has a pneumatic exhaust intended to be connected to a separate exhaust pipe this should be mentioned in the installation instructions.

96   Also, under Schedule 3 section 1.7.2 of the SM(S) Regulations, information must be supplied on any residual risk after all means of noise reduction have been incorporated in the manufacture of the machinery. This means that information must be given on the noise emissions under foreseeable use of the machinery. This information is in addition to the emission values listed in paragraph 95, which are measured under standardised test conditions.

97   The information can be provided in any convenient way which will bring it to the attention of the purchaser, for example in the instructions accompanying the machine, in catalogues or in separate data sheets.

98   A full test report might also be provided to the purchasers on request. The test report should include sufficient information to allow interpretation of the data, including:

- installation, operating and loading conditions during the test;

- the locations at which the noise was measured.

99   Where a procedure is used which is published by a recognised authority (such as the British Standards Institution (BSI), the European Standards Organisation (CEN), or the International Standards Organisation (ISO)), a reference to the standard will usually be sufficient.

Test procedures

100 Information on the noise emitted by machines is best provided on the basis of recognised test procedures under standardised conditions. This will allow the user to compare information from different machine suppliers. However, the noise levels produced by the machine in the workplace may be different from the standardised test data. For machines produced in series, the information will usually be obtained from tests of representative samples of the machine. This will need to be backed up by good quality control such as some noise checks of individual machines.

101 Where no suitable procedure is available, or if the manufacturer decides to use an alternative system of testing, a new procedure will need to be developed. Advice on the drafting of noise test codes is given in BS EN ISO 12001.[10] This document has been used to form the basis of the harmonised standards developed in support of the Machinery Directive 89/392/EEC. When a new procedure is devised, it will need to be tested to establish:

● that it provides a fair and reasonable test of all the modes of operation of the machine;

● that the results can be reproduced and repeated.

102 Whatever test procedure is used, it should be established that it provides sufficient information to meet all the requirements of the SM(S) Regulations.

103 Machine testing needs to be controlled by personnel familiar with both the acoustical procedures and the machinery being tested. Many tests require comparatively simple facilities which can be arranged at the manufacturer's or supplier's premises; others require specific facilities. In some cases it may be necessary to have the machine tested by a third party.

Labelling and marking

104 Schedule 3 section 1.7.3 of the SM(S) Regulations requires that all machinery must be labelled/marked with the following minimum information:

● the name and address of the manufacturer;

● CE marking, which includes the year of construction;

● a designation of series or type;

● a serial number, if any.

105 If it is reasonably foreseeable that the workers who use the machine will be required by the Noise Regulations to use ear protectors (ie their noise exposure will be at or above the 200 pascals peak or 90 dB(A) second action levels described in Part 1), the information should, wherever reasonably practicable, include warning signs or labels attached to the machine. The nature and content of the sign will depend on the type of machine concerned, and might for example include:

● a permanent sign, warning that ear protectors are to be used when operating the machine (see Figure 2(a));

● a removable sign for machines which produce high levels of noise in some modes of use, warning that a noise assessment will be needed after installation (see Figure 2(b));

● a removable notice saying that information on noise emission is available separately.

(a)   Example of a sign informing that ear protectors should be worn (white on a circular blue background).

(b)   Sign suitable for warning that a noise assessment will be needed after installation.

Figure 2 Safety signs

26

106 All signs should comply with the Health and Safety (Safety Signs and Signals) Regulations 1996.[11] Machines subject to legislation implementing EC Directives may be subject to special labelling requirements.

Other legislation

107 For some machines, noise emission limits have been established by law (see paragraph 88). Where these limits are intended to control noise at worker positions, compliance with them will be adequate to meet the noise reduction requirements of section 6 of the HSW Act and the SM(S) Regulations. However, the designer, manufacturer, supplier or importer should make sure that the limit is intended for this purpose; some requirements are meant to limit nuisance noise and further action might be needed to satisfy the requirements of section 6 and the SM(S) Regulations. For example, if a machine with a driver's cab is subject to an external noise limit intended to control neighbourhood nuisance, it might still be necessary to reduce the noise inside the cab to protect the operator.

How to choose a competent person - Advice for employers

Overview

- What makes a competent person?

- What skills are required to make a good assessment?

- What are the limitations of a competent person?

- How can a person be trained to be competent?

- What topics should a training course contain?

- The consultant as the competent person.

- Where can I get further information?

Introduction

108 Regulation 4(1) of the Noise Regulations requires you to ensure that a noise assessment is made by a competent person. Part 3 gives advice on what you should be looking for in a competent person and what training they should receive.

What is required of a competent person?

109 Your competent person will need to be capable of bringing together and presenting enough information about the noise exposures to enable you to make correct decisions on what you need to do to comply with regulations 7, 8, 9 and 11 of the Noise Regulations, and advising on whether you need additional specialist support. Knowledge alone will not be sufficient; the person should also possess experience and skills appropriate to the situations to be handled, including:

- the purpose of the assessments;

- a good basic understanding of what information needs to be obtained;

- an appreciation of his or her own limitations, whether of knowledge, experience, facilities or resources;

- how to make measurements;

- how to record results, analyse and explain them to others;

- the reasons for using various kinds of instrumentation and how to use and look after the instruments involved;

- how to interpret information provided by others, eg how to calculate probable noise exposures from information about the noise generated by tools when in use.

110 Your competent person will not need an advanced knowledge of acoustics. Nor will they need detailed knowledge and experience of selecting and designing control measures to complete a noise assessment, but will need to indicate to you where other further specialist assistance may be required. This means they may need an outline appreciation of further advanced topics.

111 The level of expertise needed by the competent person will depend largely on the complexity of the situation to be assessed. Where workers are regularly exposed to steady noise throughout the working day (eg in a weaving shed), or to intermittent but regular periods of steady noise (eg the operator of an automatic lathe), the task is straightforward and may only require the ability to handle simple instruments and relate their readings to the requirements of the Noise Regulations. Those who are to assess irregular exposures, or situations where workers intermittently use a variety of different machines, will need a better understanding of techniques involved in establishing daily noise exposure.

Appointing a competent person from your workforce

112 It is possible that someone in your workforce already possesses the skills, knowledge and experience necessary to undertake a noise assessment in your workplace. The ability to understand and apply this guidance in making an adequate assessment may be more important than formal qualifications. Many engineers, scientists and other technical staff may have gained sufficient skill to carry out a competent assessment through practical experience of making noise measurements and using the results. Some will, however, need further training. This may be available through short courses provided by technical colleges and other institutions.

113 A course covering the topics listed in Table 1 'Typical topics for general training courses' should provide a basis for dealing with most industrial situations, and for recognising where more specialised expertise may be needed. The course content can be expanded to prepare the competent person for a wider range of work, eg the selection

of noise control measures. All courses should include a substantial practical element, ending in an appropriate assessment of the students' practical and theoretical competence.

Availability of training

114 A variety of short training courses is available organised both on a national basis and to meet local requirements. For example, courses organised on a national basis through technical institutions include some short sessions designed to provide training for the purposes of the Noise Regulations, such as those for the Certificate of Competence in Workplace Noise Assessment of the Institute of Acoustics (IOA). Training on noise is also available in modules forming part of more general courses, such as those leading to the National Diploma in Occupational Safety and Health of the National Examination Board in Occupational Safety and Health (NEBOSH), the Certificate of Operational Competence in Comprehensive Occupational Hygiene of the British Institute of Occupational Hygienists (BIOH) and the IOA Diploma in Acoustics and Noise Control. Contact addresses for these organisations can be found in paragraph 119.

115 Where training is being arranged, its extent and coverage will depend on the technical ability of the student and whether they will be eventually expected to provide advice on measures required by other parts of the Noise Regulations as well as to make the assessments required by regulation 4. Courses covering the topics listed in Table 1 to the necessary depth would typically require 2 to 5 days, the longer time being appropriate where students would be expected to provide basic advice on straightforward measures such as the selection of ear protection, as well as assessing the noise itself.

116 To provide cost-effective advice on engineering control, the person would need to make a more thorough study of the principles of noise control engineering. Some universities and technical institutes provide specialised courses at a range of levels, and general courses on noise control engineering are available. A module in noise control engineering is available as part of the IOA Diploma in Acoustic and Noise Control.

Table 1 Typical topics for general training courses

Note: This topic list is suggested as the basis for general courses. It may need to be adjusted to suit courses intended to train people for a particular range of tasks, eg those concerned with assessments within a particular industry or company.

Topic	Essential information	Elementary introduction
Legal requirements	Noise at Work Regulations 1989	Offshore Electricity and Noise Regulations 1997
	The Health and Safety at Work etc Act 1974	Supply of Machinery (Safety) Regulations 1992 (as amended in 1994)
	Management of Health and Safety at Work Regulations 1992	Provision and Use of Work Equipment Regulations 1992
The purpose of a noise assessment	To assess exposure; to help comply with the Noise at Work Regulations 1989	
The requirement for assessments under the Noise at Work Regulations 1989	Introduction to other requirements and HSE noise guidance	Overview of other common systems for rating noise, eg noise rating (NR) curves, other weightings, their uses and limitations
	General introduction to the nature and propagation of sound	Introduction to the human ear
	Sound as a pressure wave propagated through air with a	Hearing and its measurement (audiometry)

Topic	Essential information	Elementary introduction
	simple physical model of sound generation by vibrating surfaces and vibration in fluid flow systems such as air jets	The effects of noise on hearing: permanent threshold shift (PTS), temporary threshold shift (TTS), and tinnitus. The impact of PTS and tinnitus on the individual
	Decibel scales of sound pressure and sound power	
	Sound dispersion with distance, absorption, reflection. Sound propagation in small workshops and rooms; reverberation and standing waves. Sound propagation in a large workshop with a relatively low ceiling	
	The audible frequency range and the frequency response of the human ear - dB(A)	
	The use of the dB(C) weighting as regards peak measurement	
	Daily personal noise exposure ($L_{EP,d}$) and its relation to sound level and time. Other names by which this quantity is known and related quantities such as L_{eq}, L_{ex} and Pa^2-hours	
Equipment for measuring noise	Sound level meters	Introduction to other instruments likely to be encountered, eg miniature microphones, magnetic tape recorders, real time analysers, graphic level recorders and sound intensity meters; their uses and limitations
	Integrating sound level meters; personal sound exposure meters (dosemeters) and procedures for making sure they are used properly and calibrated when required	
	Use of equipment to measure weighted, octave-band levels, L_{eq} and $L_{EP,d}$ and peak sound pressure	Use of equipment to measure SEL
	Maintenance of equipment including daily checks and periodic full calibration	
Procedures for measuring noise and noise exposure	Survey procedure	
	The practical difficulty of determining the exposure of people who move about a great deal	
	Sampling techniques and their limitations	
	Octave-band and other forms of frequency analysis	
	Microphone placement and its effect on measurement accuracy, including the effect of placing a microphone very close to a person's body	

Topic	Essential information	Elementary introduction
	Measurement of peak sound pressure levels Procedures for determining the noise exposure caused by the variable use of portable tools	
Calculation of $L_{EP,d}$	Calculation of a simple exposure from one source Calculation of a complex exposure from various sources and exposure times Normalisation of variable shift lengths to an 8-hour $L_{EP,d}$ Recording and presenting the exposure results	Interpretation of dosemeter results
Noise sources and noise control		Sources - general principles of noise generated by machinery Noise control - enclosures, exhaust silencers, damping materials and linings for chutes etc, isolation to inhibit structure-borne sound, separation of noise sources from people, cabins and enclosures around workplaces, and 'noise refuges' etc Introduction to common faults in installation; faults likely to develop in service
Ear protection	Types: reusable and disposable earplugs, earmuffs, and special types (such as protectors incorporating communication systems) Methods of using standard test data to determine the 'assumed protection' Need for protectors to be initially fitted to individuals; importance of correct use; routine checking and maintenance Hygiene and cleanliness Ways of identifying ear protection zones Ways of encouraging the correct use of ear protectors	British, European and International standards for ear protectors
Guidance literature	Introduction to sources of information available from HSE publications, and the various British, International and European standards	

Appointing a consultant as a competent person

117 You may decide that the appropriate expertise to carry out a noise assessment is not available in-house. If you choose to appoint a consultant as your competent person you will need to ensure that they have undergone training or have otherwise obtained the skills, knowledge and expertise listed in paragraphs 109-111.

118 HSE has produced a comprehensive booklet to help you select a consultant to carry out many of the tasks required by legislation. This booklet advises you when to use a consultant, what a consultancy can provide, how to choose the right consultancy and how you can judge the services they provide.[12]

119 Organisations providing training courses are:

The Institute of Acoustics (IOA)
77A St Peter's Street
St Albans
Herts AL1 3BN
Tel: 01727 848195
Fax: 01727 850553
E-Mail: Acoustics@clus1.ulcc.ac.uk

National Examining Board in Occupational Safety and Health (NEBOSH)
Industrial Relations Services Training
First Floor, Lincoln House
296-302 High Holborn
London WC1V 7SH
Tel: 0171 420 3500
Fax: 0171 420 3520

British Institute of Occupational Hygienists (BIOH)
Suite 2
Georgian House
Great Northern Road
Derby DE1 1LT
Tel: 01332 298087
Fax: 01332 298099

How to carry out a noise assessment - Advice for the competent person

Overview

Assessment

- What is the aim of a noise assessment?

- What is noise exposure?

- Who should be assessed?

- What should I do with the assessment?

- When do I need to repeat the assessment?

Measurement

- What is used to measure noise and exposure?

- Where, and how, should the measurements be made?

- How is daily noise exposure determined from the measurement of noise level?

Introduction

120   Part 4 contains advice to the competent person on measuring noise and determining the daily personal noise exposure when making a noise assessment. Employers will also find this information helpful because they are responsible for appointing the competent person. More advanced techniques than those described here may be needed when designing noise control measures or selecting ear protection.

Noise assessment

What is the aim of a noise assessment?

121   The purpose of a noise assessment is to:

- identify those people at risk from hearing damage so that the employer can formulate an action plan for controlling noise exposure in accordance with the Noise at Work Regulations 1989;

- determine the daily noise exposure ($L_{EP,d}$) of those who are likely to be exposed at or above the first action level (or the peak noise exposure of those likely to be exposed above the peak action level). **The assessment is incomplete without the $L_{EP,d}$ for those workers exposed above the first action level;**

- identify any additional information which might be needed to comply with the Noise Regulations, such as where and what type of noise control or ear protection is appropriate.

122   Additional measurements of octave-band or C-weighted levels are recommended as part of the assessment, particularly where ear protection is likely to be used as an immediate solution.

123   In all cases the noise assessment is of workers' personal noise exposure *without* ear protection.

What is noise exposure?

124   Any audible sound should be considered as noise and be part of a person's noise exposure. This includes speech, music, noise from communication devices or personal stereos, as well as the noise of machinery.

125   The daily personal noise exposure ($L_{EP,d}$) is related to the sound pressure levels to which a person is exposed and the times for which they are exposed. The $L_{EP,d}$ is a measure of the total amount of noise energy received by a person during the working day.

126   There is a risk associated with exposure to any very high sound pressure levels, usually short bursts of noise such as those from impact or explosive events. For this reason you may also need to check if the peak action level is likely to be exceeded at any time during the working day.

Who should be assessed?

127   You need to assess the exposure of all who, during the course of the working day, may receive an exposure at, or in excess of, the first or peak action levels. This includes those who spend most of the day working at a noisy location, those who may enter noisy areas for short periods, such as lift truck drivers and supervisors, and those whose noise exposure varies from day to day such as maintenance staff.

What should I do with the noise assessment?

128   It is important that after the assessment you produce a proper record. The following checklist is a guide to show the type of information you should

include in your noise assessment records. A minimum adequate record will include details of:

- the workplaces, areas, jobs or people assessed;

- measurement locations and durations and any noise control measures being used at the time;

- the work patterns and calculations of daily exposure;

- daily personal noise exposures ($L_{EP,d}$) where they are above the first action level;

- peak noise exposure levels where they are above the peak action level;

- the sources of noise;

- any further information necessary to help comply with the reduction of noise exposure;

- the date of the assessment;

- who made the assessment.

129 Additional elements that you might incorporate in the record include:

- details of the instruments used, the sensitivity calibration checks and the last periodic verification;

- a tabular record of the noise exposure resulting from various tasks or activities, identified by person, work area or operation;

- a plan showing noise levels at various places in the premises and a record of who works there and typical working times;

- a record of the type of workplace likely to be visited by employees who move about and the associated noise levels and exposures;

- recommended actions for reducing noise exposure (see paragraph 130).

130 The assessment should be the first step for the employer to develop a prioritised action plan for introducing noise control measures, incorporating:

- immediate actions to control noise exposure (eg ear protection);

- future actions to reduce noise exposure, such as:

    - the treatment of machines, processes or rooms;

    - changes to work processes, patterns and locations;

    - segregation of quiet and noisy tasks;

    - the provision of ear protection;

(More detailed noise measurements may be required to establish the requirements of these noise control measures.)

- information and training, including ear protection zone labelling and training on noise hazards and control;

- health surveillance activities;

- the name of the person responsible for carrying out the action plan;

- a date for completion of the action plan;

- the planned date for review of the assessment;

- any workplace changes which would require an update of the assessment.

131 The information recorded in a noise assessment will be dependent, among other things, on the actual work situation and the method, or methods, used for measurement of exposure. There can be no single assessment record which is suitable in all situations. Examples of suggested simple and more complex assessment records are given in Figures 5 to 13.

When do I need to repeat the assessment?

132 You will need to reassess a person's daily noise exposure when there are any changes which will alter the daily noise exposure from the value obtained in the previous assessment. Some factors that could alter the noise exposure are:

- changes in the number of hours worked in noisy places;

- changes in the work pattern;

- the introduction of different machinery or processes; and

- the implementation of noise control measures.

133 The extent of the reassessment will depend on the nature of the changes and the number of people affected by them. A change in hours or work patterns may require a recalculation of the noise exposure for the people affected, but no further measurements. The introduction of new machinery or processes may require a full reassessment of an area. The use of ear protectors, or a change in the type of ear protector, does not affect the assessed noise exposure.

134 In addition it is worthwhile making regular repeat checks of the levels of noise, ideally at least once every two years. If changes are found, the exposure assessment for those affected by the change in level will need to be repeated.

Noise measurement

What do I use to measure noise?

135 The basic instrument is a sound level meter. A dosemeter (personal sound exposure meter) worn by the employee can also be used. Dual-purpose instruments are also available which can operate as both sound level meters and dosemeters. A calibrator to check the meter accuracy and a windshield to protect the microphone against air movement and dirt are essential accessories.

136 Other more sophisticated equipment such as data recorders, frequency analysers and sound intensity analysers can be used for a more detailed assessment. This equipment is not covered by this guide.

Sound level meters

137 The basic instrument for carrying out a noise assessment is likely to be an integrating sound level meter capable of the following measurements:

- A-weighted L_{eq};

- C-weighted maximum peak sound pressure levels, to above 140 dB(C).★

138 The following additional features may also be needed for prescribing ear protection and noise control measures:

- C-weighted L_{eq};

- octave-band analysis.

139 Where the sound pressure level is steady for long periods, non-integrating sound level meters, which give a simple indication of A-weighted sound pressure level, may be used for noise assessments. Where the sound pressure level is not steady, an integrating sound level meter is essential.

Dosemeters

40 Where a person is highly mobile or working in places where access for the measurement is

difficult, a dosemeter is an alternative means of measuring a person's noise exposure. However, the microphone is worn on the body so there is very likely to be an additional uncertainty to dosemeter measurements because of extra local noise disturbance.

141 Dosemeters indicate the total noise dose received over the measurement period in Pascal squared hours (Pa^2.h)† or as a percentage of an $L_{EP,d}$ (usually 85 or 90 dB(A)). Modern meters are required to provide a means of converting the reading to Pa^2.h, if this is not directly indicated on the meter.

142 Many dosemeters have additional features. Those which record how the sound pressure level varies with time throughout the measurement can be useful to show when and where high noise exposures occur.

143 All dosemeter measurements should be made with a 3 dB exchange rate (sometimes called the doubling rate). Some dosemeters include additional 4 and 5 dB exchange rates to meet American standards; these should not be used for noise exposure assessments.

Calibrators

144 A sound calibrator should be used to check the meter accuracy each day before and after making any measurements. Calibrators give a tone at a specified sound pressure level and frequency for a specified microphone type using an appropriate adaptor. Make sure you have the right calibrator with the right adaptors for your microphone.

145 Some meters have an internal electronic calibration. The internal calibration only checks the accuracy of the instrument electronics and does not provide a check of the meter's microphone. However, it can be a useful cross-check of the accuracy of the meter and calibrator.

What grade of instrument do I need?

146 Your sound level meter, dosemeter or calibrator should meet the applicable European standards listed in Appendix 1. Sound level meters and calibrators are also graded by class or type. The lower the type or class number, the more accurate the instrument is. Use at least a Type 2 or Class 2 sound level meter and Class 2 calibrator for a noise assessment. Dosemeters have no type or class number.

★ While it is recommended that peak levels are measured with C-weighting, for noises which have energy components at both the high and low frequency ends of the noise spectrum (0-20 Hz and greater than 15 kHz) possible errors could occur. In these extreme situations, you may need to seek expert advice.

†A measure of the total sound energy received during a measurement period. The $L_{EP,d}$ may be calculated from this dose value (see worked examples 5 and 6 in Appendix 4).

Peak sound pressure level

147 If your instrument has no peak indication, you can check the peak sound pressure level by measuring the A-weighted sound pressure level with an F (fast) response. If the maximum reading is below 125 dB(A) the maximum peak level is likely to be below the 140 dB(C) peak action level.

148 Often sound level meters include an 'I' (impulse) response. This cannot be used for any measurements that are part of a noise assessment.

Periodic testing of instruments

149 Both your meter and calibrator need to have been tested in the previous two years to ensure they still meet the required standards. If your equipment is more than two years old, check you have a test certificate confirming the performance of your meter *and* calibrator before you start your assessment. Appendix 1 gives more details on periodic testing.

Where should I measure, and how should the measurements be made?

Where?

150 When assessing a person's noise exposure, make measurements at every location that they work in or pass through during the working day, and note the time spent at each location. It is generally not necessary to record exposures to sound pressure levels below 80 dB(A), since such exposures are not significant in relation to the daily noise exposure action levels.

151 Operators may need to be present while the measurements are made, for example to control the machine. Measurements should be made with the microphone positioned close enough to the operator's head to obtain a reliable assessment of the noise to which they are exposed, but preferably not so close that reflections cause errors. The results are unlikely to be significantly affected by reflections if the microphone is kept at least 4 cm away from an operator. The microphone should be placed on the side where the noise levels are higher.

152 To avoid making large numbers of measurements, for example where the sound pressure level is changing, or if the person is moving within a noisy area, it is advisable to assume the worst case and measure at the noisiest location, or during the loudest periods. If the assessment shows the daily personal noise exposure is above the action level, then, if necessary, the worst-case assumption may be reviewed.

153 If you are using a dosemeter to measure a person's noise exposure, position the microphone on the shoulder and prevent it touching the neck, rubbing on, or being covered by, clothing or protective equipment. If the dosemeter body is connected to the microphone by a flexible cable, place it securely in a pocket or on a belt where it can be safe from damage during the measurement.

How long?

154 The noise level to which an individual employee is exposed will normally change throughout the day because, for example, different machines or materials might be used at different times. You must take sufficient noise measurements to account for all these changes, recording the sound level and the person's exposure time at each noise level.

155 With a sound level meter, you need to measure at each position or during each task, long enough to obtain an indication of the average level the person is exposed to. You may need to measure the A-weighted L_{eq} for the entire period but usually a shorter measurement is sufficient. In general:

- if the noise is steady, a short sound pressure level or A-weighted L_{eq} measurement may be enough;

- if the noise is changing, wait for the A-weighted L_{eq} reading to settle to within 1 dB;

- if the noise is from a cyclic operation, measure the A-weighted L_{eq} over a whole number of cycles.

156 The time required depends on the nature of the work. A reading may take just 20 seconds or several hours.

157 Noise dosemeters are designed to operate for longer periods. They are ideal for measurements over an entire shift, or for a period of several hours during a shift. If you measure over part of a shift, make sure the period is long enough to be typical of the rest of the working day, so that you can reliably predict the full daily exposure. Avoid very short measurements, as these may only give a very low dose reading which can be inaccurate due to the limited resolution of the dosemeter's display. Also make sure that the dose reading relates to actual true noise exposure, not false input from unrepresentative noise sources when the meter is not supervised, for example artificial bangs, whistling, blowing and tampering with the microphone.

Sample measurements for a group

158 If several workers work in the same area, you may be able to assess the exposure for them all from measurements in selected locations. When making the assessment, choose the locations and times spent in each place so that you determine the highest exposure that someone is likely to receive.

Mobile workers and highly variable daily exposures

159 For some jobs (such as maintenance) the work and the noise exposure will vary from day to day so there is no typical daily exposure. For people in these jobs, measurements need to be made of the range of activities undertaken, possibly over several days. From these the worst likely daily exposure should be estimated.

Measurements close to the ear

160 Measurements of noise very close to the ear, such as sound from a communication headset worn under a motor cycle helmet, require specialist equipment and procedures. Appendix 2 gives further information.

How do I determine noise exposure?

161 If you have used a sound level meter you will have measurements of the sound pressure level or the sound pressure level averaged over a representative period (the A-weighted L_{eq}) at the different places a person works and for the different tasks carried out during the day. The daily exposure or $L_{EP,d}$ is calculated from these values and the time spent in each place or at each task measured. It is important that you have the correct exposure times, especially for the periods spent in the highest sound levels, even if the time is only very short.

162 The $L_{EP,d}$ can be calculated using the following method:

Step 1 Determine fractional noise exposure values for each noise exposure, which is given by:
$$f = \frac{t}{8} \text{ antilog } [0.1(L - 90)]$$

where, t is the exposure time in hours and L is the sound pressure level or A-weighted L_{eq}.

Step 2 Add together the fractional exposure values to give a total fractional exposure, f_T.

Step 3 Determine the daily noise exposure, given by: $L_{EP,d} = 90 + 10 \log f_T$.

163 The method may be carried out by a simple nomogram (see Figure 3), or using a calculator. Worked examples are given in Appendices 3 and 4, showing how daily noise exposures are determined using both nomogram and calculation methods for noise levels measured using both sound level meters (Appendix 3) and dosemeters (Appendix 4).

164 The fractional exposures from a series of noise sources can be used by the employer to prioritise noise control activities. The highest fractional exposure values are given by the machines or processes which make the greatest contributions to daily noise exposure. Therefore, tackling these noise sources will have the greatest effect on personal noise exposures.

Short-duration noise

165 For some short-duration noises such as gunfire, explosions and cartridge-operated tools where the noise is associated with discrete events, the noise exposure from the number of events in the day can be calculated from the measured SEL (sound exposure level). SEL is the equivalent level if all the noise had occurred in 1 second.

166 The fractional exposure value for the short-duration noise is given by:

$$f = \frac{n}{m} \text{ antilog } [0.1(\text{SEL} - 134.6)]$$

where n is the number of times the noise event occurs per working day and m is the number of times the noise event occurred during the SEL measurement (in many cases m will equal 1). The nomogram in Figure 4 may be used to determine this fractional exposure value.

167 The fractional exposure from the short-duration noise may be added to fractional exposure values from other sources to give the total fractional exposure value, from which the daily noise exposure may be determined. Appendix 5 shows how SEL may be used to determine daily noise exposure using the nomogram at Figure 4 or a calculator.

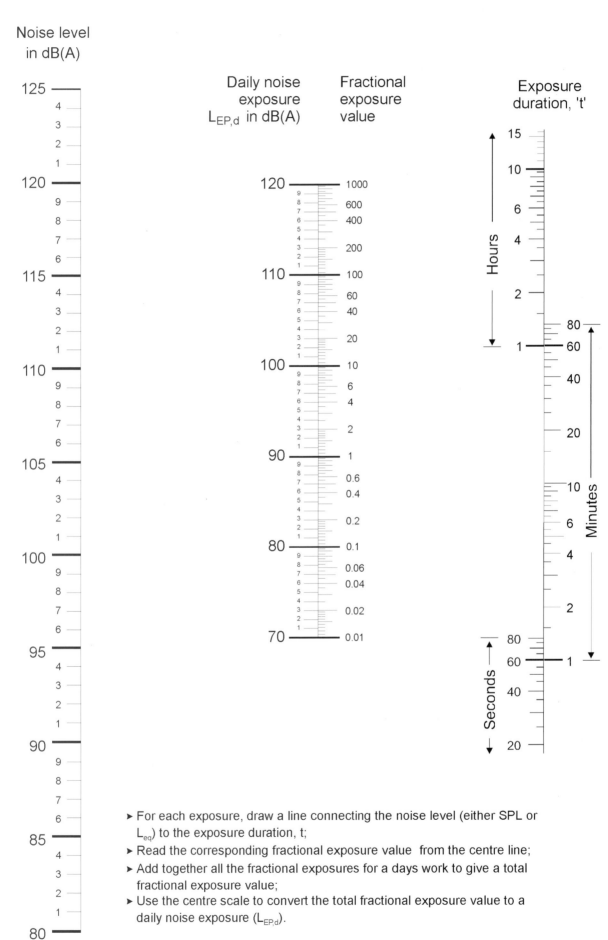

Figure 3 Nomogram for determining fractional exposures from A-weighted SPL or A-weighted L_{eq} and exposure times

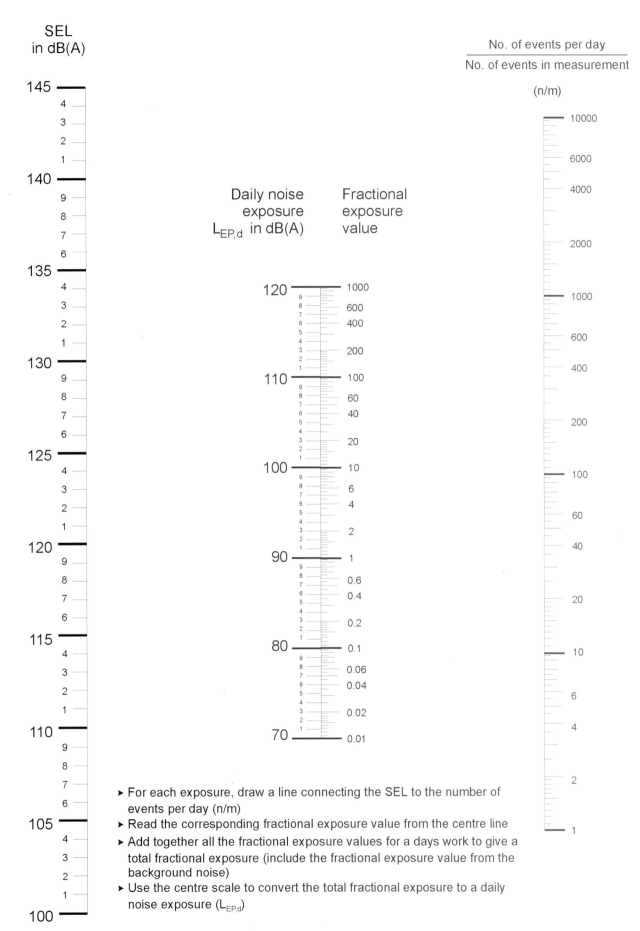

SEL in dB(A)

No. of events per day / No. of events in measurement (n/m)

Daily noise exposure $L_{EP,d}$ in dB(A)

Fractional exposure value

► For each exposure, draw a line connecting the SEL to the number of events per day (n/m)
► Read the corresponding fractional exposure value from the centre line
► Add together all the fractional exposure values for a days work to give a total fractional exposure (include the fractional exposure value from the background noise)
► Use the centre scale to convert the total fractional exposure to a daily noise exposure ($L_{EP,d}$)

Figure 4 Nomogram for determining fractional exposures from the SEL and number of events

Figure 5 Worked example of a simple assessment report

This assessment was carried out by John Smith. It is for employee R E Brown who works principally at four locations, three around the widget swathing machine and one in the packaging area.

The assessment report gives information on the employee, the instrumentation used for the noise measurements, the noise exposures and recommendations for controlling exposure, both immediately and in the future.

The report shows that R E Brown is exposed above the first and second action levels, but not the peak action level. An interim recommendation is made for wearing ear protection, although the assessment does not have sufficient information to say what sort. A recommendation for controlling the machine noise in the future is also given.

NOISE ASSESSMENT

Employee:	R E Brown
Job title:	Widget swaging machine operator
Date of assessment:	31 June 1998

Instrumentation details

Meter model/type number:	SLM type S123	*Serial number:*	A 1234
Date of meter's last verification:			29 Feb 1998
Calibrator type:	SLM type C456	*Serial number:*	A 1235
Calibration level and frequency:	94 dB @1000 Hz	*Date of calibrator's last verification:*	29 Feb 1998

Noise exposure assessments

Noise sources	*Sound pressure level L_A dB(A)*	*Exposure times (hours/minutes)*	*Fractional exposures*	*Peak SPL dB(C)*
Widget swaging machine:				
operator position	97	4 hrs	2.506	126
widget collection point	86	30 mins	0.025	101
swaging preparation	93	1 hr 30 mins	0.374	115
Packaging area:				
widget wrapper	82	1 hr 20 mins	0.026	93
Total fractional exposure:			2.931	
Total daily exposure $L_{EP,d}$ dB(A):			94.7	
Action level exceeded?	$L_{EP,d}$:			**Peak:**
	85 dB ✔	90 dB(A) ✔		140 dB(C) (200 Pa) ☐

Recommendations for action

Immediate:	Make the area around the widget making machine an ear protection zone - suitable protection to be identified.
Future:	To provide a suitable noise enclosure for the swager. Note: this may also provide protection from debris, therefore eye protection will no longer be required

Assessed by:	J A Smith		
Signature:	*John A Smith*	**Date:**	31 June 1998

There are no blank assessment record forms included in this guidance since the format of the record will depend on the situation. If you wish you may use the format shown here as a basis for your own noise assessment record.

Figure 6 Assessment report example for a small work area - general information

This example extends that in Figure 5 to show how measurements at one location might affect more than one employee. This example is for the whole workforce of F B Jones and Son. The general details of the assessment are recorded on this first page.

GENERAL INFORMATION

Company details

Name:	F B Jones & Son
Address:	Factory Lane Widget Town Widgetshire AB1 2CD
Business activity:	Processing widgets
Number of employees:	3
Person responsible for noise assessment:	C F Jones
Tel:	0123 456 7890

Assessment details

Area or areas to be assessed:	Preparation and packaging
Number of employees:	2
Number of machines or work locations:	2

Assessor details

Name:	J A Smith
Company:	JAS Consultants
Address:	Noise Street Widget Town Widgetshire AB1 3CD
Tel:	0123 456 7891
Signature:	John A Smith
Date of assessment:	31 June 1998

There are no blank assessment record forms included in this guidance since the format of the record will depend on the situation. If you wish you may use the format shown here as a basis for your own noise assessment record.

Figure 7   Assessment report example for a small work area - Area noise measurements

The following four report forms are the area noise measurements for the positions occupied by the two employees during the working day. Each report form provides an opportunity to record additional information, such as the octave-band information and C-weighted L_{eq} recorded here. This information may be of use for noise control or ear protection selection.

AREA NOISE MEASUREMENTS							*No:*	1

Area details

Machine/area:	Widget swaging machine, preparation area
Process/activity:	Machine operation
Measurement location:	Operator position
Who is exposed to noise at this location:	R E Brown - Widget swaging machine operator
	S E Lee - Packer
Measurement date:	31 June 1998

Sound level meter details

Meter model/type number:	SLM type S123B	*Serial number:*	A 1236
Date of meter's last full verification:			29 Feb 98

On-site calibration

Calibrator type:	SLM type C123	*Serial number:*	A 1235
Date of calibrator's last full verification:			29 Feb 98
Calibration level:	94 *dB*	*Calibration frequency:*	1000 *Hz*

Exposure assessment measurements

Description of measurement period (eg no. of work cycles):	Swaging of 20 widgets		
A-weighted L_{eq} (L_A):	97 *dB(A)* *Measurement duration:*	15 minutes
SEL_A:	N/A *dB(A)* *No. of events:*	N/A
Max peak SPL:	126 *dB(C)*	

Other information

Frequency (Hz):	63	125	250	500	1000	2000	4000	8000
Octave-band SPL (dB):	85	86	94	95	90	89	86	89

C-weighted L_{eq} (L_C):	99 *dB(C)*	*(L_C - L_A =*	2 *dB)*
SEL_C:	*dB(C)*	*(SEL_C - SEL_A =*	*dB)*
$L_{A,fast,max}$:	*dB(A)*		
$L_{C,fast,max}$:	*dB(C)*	*($L_{C,fast,max}$ - $L_{A,fast,max}$ =*	*dB)*
Measured by:	J A Smith		
Signature:	*John A Smith*		
Date:	31 June 1998		

There are no blank assessment record forms included in this guidance since the format of the record will depend on the situation. If you wish you may use the format shown here as a basis for your own noise assessment record.

Figure 8 Assessment report example for a small work area - Area noise measurements (continued)

AREA NOISE MEASUREMENTS			*No:*	2

Area details

Machine/area:	Widget swaging machine, packaging area
Process/activity:	Machine idling
Measurement location:	Collection point
Who is exposed to noise at this location:	R E Brown - Widget swaging machine operator
	S E Lee - Packer
Measurement date:	31 June 1998

Sound level meter details

Meter model/type number:	SLM type S123B	*Serial number:*	A 1236
Date of meter's last full verification:			29 Feb 98

On-site calibration

Calibrator type:	SLM type C123	*Serial number:*	A 1235
Date of calibrator's last full verification:			29 Feb 98
Calibration level:	94 *dB*	*Calibration frequency:*	1000 *Hz*

Exposure assessment measurements

Description of measurement period (eg number of work cycles):	Collection of widgets from delivery tray (machine idling)				
A-weighted L_{eq} (L_A):	86	*dB(A)*	*Measurement duration:*	5 minutes	
SEL_A:	N/A	*dB(A)*	*No of events:*	N/A	
Max peak SPL:	101	*dB(C)*			

Additional information

Frequency (Hz):	63	125	250	500	1000	2000	4000	8000
Octave-band SPL (dB):	78	82	80	82	80	78	77	79

C-weighted L_{eq} (L_C):	89	*dB(C)*	(L_C - L_A =	3	*dB*)
SEL_C:		*dB(C)*	(SEL_C - SEL_A =		*dB*)
$L_{A,fast,max}$:		*dB(A)*			
$L_{C,fast,max}$:		*dB(C)*	($L_{C,fast,max}$ - $L_{A,fast,max}$ =		*dB*)
Measured by:	J A Smith				
Signature:	John A Smith				
Date:	31 June 1998				

There are no blank assessment record forms included in this guidance since the format of the record will depend on the situation. If you wish you may use the format shown here as a basis for your own noise assessment record.

Figure 9 Assessment report example for a small work area - Area noise measurements (continued)

AREA NOISE MEASUREMENTS							*No:*	3

Area details

Machine/area:	Widget swaging machine, preparation area
Process/activity:	Machine preparation
Measurement location:	Swaging preparation point
Who is exposed to noise at this location:	R E Brown - Widget swaging machine operator
Measurement date:	31 June 1998

Sound level meter details

Meter model/type number:	SLM type S123B	*Serial number:*	A 1236
Date of meter's last full verification:			29 Feb 98

On-site calibration

Calibrator type:	SLM type C123	*Serial number:*	A 1235
Date of calibrator's last full verification:			29 Feb 98
Calibration level:	94 *dB*	*Calibration frequency:*	1000 *Hz*

Exposure assessment measurements

Description of measurement period (eg number of work cycles):	Machine idling		
A-weighted L_{eq} (L_A):	93 *dB(A)*	*Measurement duration:*	5 minutes
SEL_A:	N/A *dB(A)*	*No. of events:*	N/A
Max peak SPL:	101 *dB(C)*		

Additional information

Frequency (Hz):	63	125	250	500	1000	2000	4000	8000
Octave-band SPL (dB):	84	86	85	88	87	86	83	87

C-weighted L_{eq} (L_C):	95 *dB(C)*	*(L_C - L_A =*	2 *dB)*
SEL_C:	*dB(C)*	*(SEL_C - SEL_A =*	*dB)*
$L_{A,fast,max}$:	*dB(A)*		
$L_{C,fast,max}$:	*dB(C)*	*($L_{C,fast,max}$ - $L_{A,fast,max}$ =*	*dB)*
Measured by:	J A Smith		
Signature:	*John A Smith*		
Date:	31 June 1998		

There are no blank assessment record forms included in this guidance since the format of the record will depend on the situation. If you wish you may use the format shown here as a basis for your own noise assessment record.

Figure 10 Assessment report example for a small work area - Area noise measurements (continued)

| AREA NOISE MEASUREMENTS | | | | | | *No:* | 4 | |

Area details

Machine/area:	Packaging area
Process/activity:	Packer
Measurement location:	Packaging point
Who is exposed to noise at this location:	S E Lee - Packer
	R E Brown - Widget swaging machine operator
Measurement date:	31 June 1998

Sound level meter details

Meter model/type number:	SLM type S123B	*Serial number:*	A 1236
Date of meter's last full verification:			29 Feb 98

On-site calibration

Calibrator type:	SLM type C123		*Serial number:*	A 1235	
Date of calibrator's last full verification:				29 Feb 98	
Calibration level:	94	*dB*	*Calibration frequency:*	1000	*Hz*

Exposure assessment measurements

Description of measurement period (eg number of work cycles):	Normal packing, during the swaging of 20 widgets (main noise source)		
A-weighted L_{eq} (L_A):	82 *dB(A)*	*Measurement duration:*	15 minutes
SEL_A:	N/A *dB(A)*	*Number of events:*	N/A
Max peak SPL:	93 *dB(C)*		

Additional information

Frequency (Hz):	*63*	*125*	*250*	*500*	*1000*	*2000*	*4000*	*8000*
Octave-band SPL (dB):	74	75	79	80	75	74	73	72

C-weighted L_{eq} (L_C):	85 *dB(C)*	*(L_C - L_A =*	3	*dB)*
SEL_C:	*dB(C)*	*(SEL_C - SEL_A =*		*dB)*
$L_{A,fast,max}$:	*dB(A)*			
$L_{C,fast,max}$:	*dB(C)*	*($L_{C,fast,max}$ - $L_{A,fast,max}$ =*		*dB)*
Measured by:	J A Smith			
Signature:	John A Smith			
Date:	31 June 1998			

There are no blank assessment record forms included in this guidance since the format of the record will depend on the situation. If you wish you may use the format shown here as a basis for your own noise assessment record.

Figure 11 Assessment report example for a small work area - Exposure assessment

The following two report forms are the exposure assessments for the two employees. The exposure assessment identifies all the noise sources relevant to the employee and their exposure times, so that fractional exposures and the $L_{EP,d}$ values can be determined.

EXPOSURE ASSESSMENT				*No:*	1

Employee:	R E Brown
Job title:	Widget swaging machine operator
Date of assessment:	31 June 1998

Area noise exposure assessments

Noise sources	*Sound pressure level L_A dB(A)*	*Exposure times*	*Fractional exposures*	*Peak SPLdB(C)*
Widget swaging machine:				
Operator position (area noise measurement 1)	97	4 hours	2.506	126
Widget collection point (area noise measurement 2)	86	30 minutes	0.025	101
Swaging preparation (area noise measurement 3)	93	1 hour 30 minutes	0.374	115
Packaging area:				
Widget wrapper (area noise measurement 4)	82	1 hour 20 minutes	0.026	93

Total fractional exposure:	2.931
Total daily exposure $L_{EP,d}$ dB(A):	94.7

Dosemeter assessment

Meter type:		*Serial number:*	
Date of meter's last full verification:			

On-site calibration

Calibrator type:		*Serial number:*	
Date of calibrator's last full verification:			
Calibration level:	*dB*	*Frequency (Hz):*	

Exposure assessment

Dose:	*Pa^2.h*
Measurement duration:	*hours*
Shift length:	*hours*
Daily noise exposure:	*dB(A)*
Assessed by:	J A Smith
Signature:	*John A Smith*
Date:	31 June 1998

There are no blank assessment record forms included in this guidance since the format of the record will depend on the situation. If you wish you may use the format shown here as a basis for your own noise assessment record.

Figure 12 Assessment report example for a small work area - Exposure assessment (continued)

EXPOSURE ASSESSMENT				*No:*	2

Employee:	S E Lee
Job title:	Packer
Date of assessment:	31 June 1998

Area noise exposure assessments

Noise sources	Sound pressure level L_A dB(A)	Exposure times	Fractional exposures	Peak SPL dB(C)
Packaging area:				
Widget wrapper (area noise measurement 4)	82	7 hours 30 minutes	0.149	93
Widget swaging machine:				
Operator position (area noise measurement 1)	97	10 minutes	0.104	126
Total fractional exposure:			0.253	
Total daily exposure $L_{EP,d}$ *dB(A):*			84	

Dosemeter assessment

Meter type:		*Serial number:*	
Date of meter's last full verification:			

On-site calibration

Calibrator type:		*Serial number:*	
Date of calibrator's last full verification:			
Calibration level:	*dB*	*Frequency (Hz):*	

Exposure assessment

Dose:	$Pa^2.h$
Measurement duration:	*hours*
Shift length:	*hours*
Daily noise exposure:	*dB(A)*
Assessed by:	J A Smith
Signature:	John A Smith
Date:	31 June 1998

There are no blank assessment record forms included in this guidance since the format of the record will depend on the situation. If you wish you may use the format shown here as a basis for your own noise assessment record.

Figure 13 Assessment report example for a small work area - Recommendations

Finally the recommended actions from the noise assessment. This form identifies recommended noise control measures and their priorities. In these recommendations, the detail provided in the noise measurements (Figures 7-10) allows better advice on ear protection to be given (using the SNR selection method - see Part 6 of this book).

Although the previous forms in this sequence would be completed by the competent person, the employer may wish the form also to be signed by a manager who has the authority to implement the recommendations of the assessment.

RECOMMENDATIONS

Noise exposure control measures

Machine/employee	Action	Action by (date)	Priority
Widget swaging machine	An acoustic enclosure, with viewing port, to reduce the noise at the operator position by 7 dB(A) (this would also provide protection from debris, so eye protection would no longer be required).	31 June 1999	High
Widget swaging machine	Additional noise control may be required to specifically reduce the noise exposure during swaging preparation. Further assessment following installation of enclosure.	31 June 1999	Medium

Immediate control measures

Employee/area	Action	Noise exposure with control measure ($L_{EP,d}$ in dB(A), or Peak SPL in dB(C))
Widget swaging machine	An ear protection zone should be created around the widget swaging machine. Ear protectors of SNR between 14 and 19 dB are recommended. This will reduce the existing sound pressure level of 97 dB(C) to between 80 and 85 dB(A).	A-weighted L_{eq} reduced to less than 85 dB(A) at operating position. Fractional exposure reduced to less than 0.16. $L_{EP,d}$ estimated to be below 84 dB(A).

Recommendations by:

Name:	J A Smith
Signature:	John A Smith
Date:	31 June 1998

Recommendations accepted by:

Name:	C F Jones
Position:	Production manager
Signature:	Clinton F Jones
Date:	31 June 1998

There are no blank assessment record forms included in this guidance since the format of the record will depend on the situation. If you wish you may use the format shown here as a basis for your own noise assessment record.

Control of noise exposure - Advice for employers and engineers

Overview

- What is noise control?

- What are the mechanisms of noise control?

- How do I formulate a noise purchasing policy for buying machines?

- How can I reduce the noise generated from an existing machine or process?

- What is active noise control?

- How can a noise transmission path be treated?

- Where can I get training in noise control?

Introduction

168 Part 5 provides outline advice on the control of noise at work. It should be read in conjunction with the general advice given in Part 1 under the guidance on regulation 7. Not all the answers to noise control are dealt with in this part. For practical examples of noise control methods, see HSE's publication *Sound solutions*, a book of case studies[6] from a wide variety of industries.

169 There are several ways noise exposure can be controlled, for example:

- design of workplaces for low noise emission;

- substitution or replacement of existing processes or machines with quieter alternatives;

- engineering control of existing noisy machines;

- modifications to the noise transmission paths;

- changes in methods of working.

Design of workplaces for low noise emission

Design of workplaces

170 When considering a new workplace (ie a greenfield site), noise emissions and noise exposure can be limited by careful choice of design, layout and the construction materials used for the

building. For example, the appropriate use of absorption materials within the building can reduce or limit the effects of reflected sound (see Figures 14 and 15).

171 Careful planning could segregate noisy machines from other areas where quiet operations are carried out (see Figure 16) reducing the need for noise control after the workplace is in operation.

172 There is a guidance document in the form of an International Standard* dealing with all aspects of design for low-noise workplaces.

Substitution of a quieter process or machine

Alternative processes

173 Changes in technology can alter the machine or process resulting in a lower noise exposure to the workforce. Sometimes a different way of working might avoid the need for a noisy operation. Some changes may produce better quality control, design and manufacturing procedures, reducing the need for noisy assembly practices and the need to rectify faults, which can save you money. Examples of quieter processes, machines and activities include:

Process change

- the use of break-stem rivets instead of hot rivets set by traditional noisy hammering;

- the use of welded instead of riveted construction in large-scale fabrications;

Change of machine

- hydraulic pressing of bearings into a casting instead of being driven in by hammering;

- replacing manual turning lathes with computer-controlled automatic machines on repetitive production;

Change of activity

- more accurate cutting of steel plate may eliminate noisy rectification processes, such as the removal of excess material by using compressed air chisels;

- replacing noisy compressed air tools with hydraulic alternatives.

* ISO 11690 *Acoustics - Recommended practice for the design of low-noise workplaces containing machinery* (Parts 1-3).

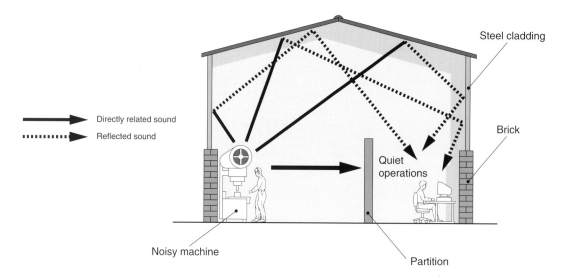

Figure 14   Noise paths found in a workplace. The quiet area is subjected to reflected noise from a machine elsewhere in the building

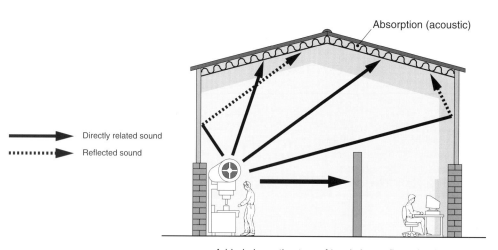

Added absorption to roof 'soaks' up reflected noise

Figure 15   The correct use of absorption in the roof will reduce the reflected noise reaching the quiet area

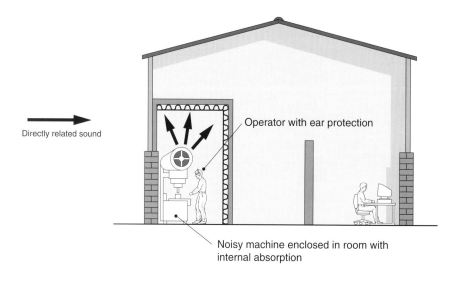

Figure 16   Segregation of the noisy operation will benefit the whole workplace

Choice of machines

174 By purchasing low-noise machines through a positive purchasing policy, expensive retrofitting of noise control measures can be avoided.

Low-noise machines

175 Machines can be designed to generate less noise, for example:

- improved design of fans, fan casings and compressors and their accurate matching to the systems they supply;

- attention to the rigidity of structural parts of machines to reduce vibration and the consequent radiated noise.

Purchasing policies

176 Often the single most cost-effective, long-term measure you can take to reduce noise at work is to introduce a purchasing policy for choosing quieter machinery. HSE has published a leaflet[7] offering advice to purchasers of noisy machinery (see also paragraphs 49-52 of Part 1 of this book).

177 Your positive noise reduction purchasing policy could involve:

- preparing a machine specification. Draw your suppliers' attention to the requirements of the Supply of Machinery (Safety) Regulations 1992, as amended in 1994 (see Part 2 of this book);

- introducing your own company 'noise limit', ie a realistic low noise emission level that you are prepared to accept from incoming plant and equipment given your circumstances and planned machine use;

- requiring a statement from all tenderers or suppliers saying if their machinery will meet your company 'noise limit' specification;

- where it is necessary to purchase 'noisy' machinery, keeping a record of the reasons for decisions made to help with the preparation of future machine specifications with information on where improvements are necessary;

- using an agreed format for the presentation of results by suppliers;

- discussing your machinery needs and noise emission levels with your safety or employee representatives(s);

- introducing a general long-term policy to reduce noise emission levels in your workplace.

Engineering control

178 The noise in any workplace can originate from one or more machines, with each machine having several noise sources. For example in a power press, the following sources may be found:

- the noise from the press tool;

- air ejection of the components;

- clutch squeal;

- component discharge.

179 Also, services such as duct extraction systems can make a considerable contribution to the overall noise exposure in the workplace. It is good practice to establish the contribution from all sources in the total noise field, and to establish which is the most dominant. Figure 17 shows how a typical machine might have several noise sources which need to be treated.

180 Methods of limiting noise generation are given in paragraphs 181-206.

Avoiding impacts

181 Try to avoid impacts, or make arrangements to cushion them, for example:

- fit buffers on stops and rubber or plastic surface coatings on chutes, to avoid metal to metal impacts;

- apply a progressive cutting edge to punch tooling on power presses to reduce the impact noise;

- use conveyor systems, designed to prevent the components being transported from impacting against each other.

182 Limit or reduce the 'drop heights' of components. Components which are produced by pressings and are ejected and then dropped into a collecting bin can cause high noise levels. Reducing the force of the impact can reduce the noise levels.

FRONT

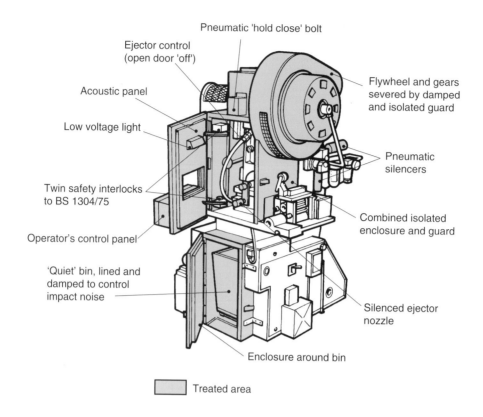

Pneumatic 'hold close' bolt

Ejector control
(open door 'off')

Acoustic panel

Low voltage light

Twin safety interlocks
to BS 1304/75

Operator's control panel

'Quiet' bin, lined and
damped to control
impact noise

Flywheel and gears
severed by damped
and isolated guard

Pneumatic
silencers

Combined isolated
enclosure and guard

Silenced ejector
nozzle

Enclosure around bin

☐ Treated area

REAR

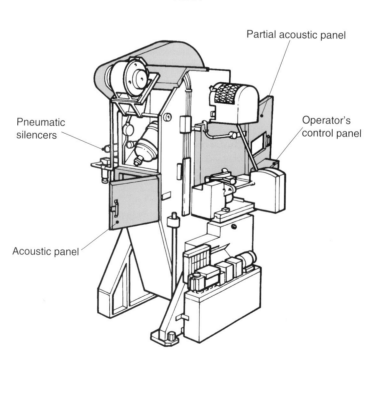

Partial acoustic panel

Pneumatic
silencers

Operator's
control panel

Acoustic panel

☐ Treated area

Figure 17   Typical noise sources on a press and some forms of treatment combined with a safety guard

Damping

183 Damping involves adding material to reduce induced vibrations and the tendency of machine parts to 'ring'. Examples of damping methods are:

● apply treatments to sheet metal, such as surface coatings or a constrained layer technique of bonding two sheets together;

● use materials such as sound-deadened steel with high damping capacity in the construction of machine casings;

● attach damping plates with bolts or spot welds to increase friction damping;

● bolt together, instead of welding, the individual steel plates joined to produce large structures;

● apply temporary damping to sheet metal work during fabrication, and to components which tend to 'squeal' while being machined.

Abrasion-resistant rubber bonded to steel plate

Steel fixing plate

Concrete slab

Post-installation plug

Concrete fixing bolt

Figure 18   By lining the surface of a distribution yard with durable rubber, the impact noise from the dropping barrels is reduced

53

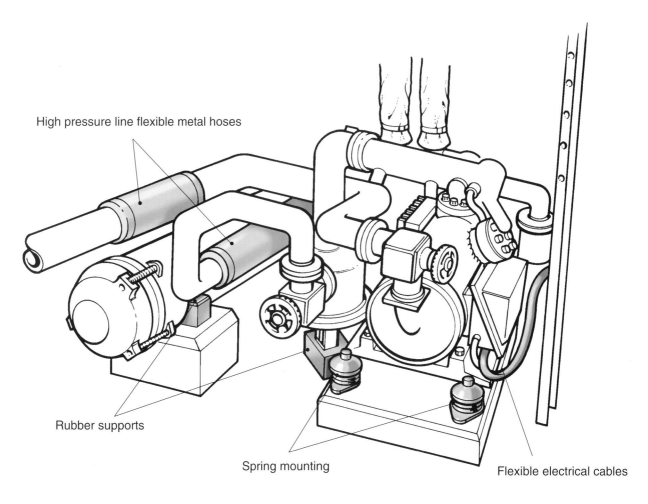

High pressure line flexible metal hoses

Rubber supports

Spring mounting

Flexible electrical cables

Figure 19   A compressor unit with isolation under the machine and on the outlet pipework

Figure 20   A porous silencer for use on compressed air exhausts

Isolation

184 Isolation involves separating the machine from its surroundings. Flexible isolators made of rubber or springs can be used to reduce the spread of structure-borne sound through a machine frame, for example:

● isolate the bearings from a gearbox case to reduce the transmission of gear noise;

● mount machines on the correct anti-vibration mounts to reduce the transmitted vibration into the structure of the workplace which if not treated may be radiated as noise;

● fit anti-vibration mountings to reduce the transmission of sound from hydraulic power supply pipes to the cab floor on an earth-moving machine.

185 Anti-vibration mountings under machines are not usually very effective for reducing noise close to a machine, unless the floor on which it stands is unusually flexible, eg mezzanine floors, but they can be effective in reducing structure-borne noise causing nuisance in nearby areas/rooms and workstations.

Silencers

186 Silencers are attachments fitted to the inlet or exhaust (or both) of a moving air or gas stream emitted from machines.

Pipes and ducts

187 Mufflers or silencers can reduce noise transmitted along pipes and ducts, for example:

● exhaust and intake silencers on internal combustion engines;

● duct silencers to control noise from exhaust ventilation fans.

Air exhausts and jets

188 Silencers can reduce noise generated by turbulence at air exhausts and jets, for example:

● a porous silencer for the exhaust of a pneumatic cylinder (see Figure 20);

● a silencer for the air supply to a shot-blaster's helmet.

● use of low noise air nozzles (see Figure 21) on pneumatic ejectors and cleaning guns constructed on good aerodynamic principles, or substitution of an alternative method of doing the job;

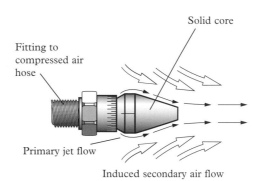

Figure 21   Induced flow nozzle

189 You should ensure that the quantity and pressure of compressed air supplied to equipment is matched to its needs. This can be achieved by providing each item of equipment with its own pressure-reducing valve. The air supply can be individually adjusted for a good compromise between reliable operation and noise. This has an added benefit of reducing the costs of the supply of compressed air.

Air turbulence noise

190 When any rotating part, such as a fan blade or a woodworking cutter block, passes close to a stationary part of the machine the resulting impact turbulence produces noise. If the distance between the rotating part and the stationary part is increased, the noise level will be reduced. Increases in the distances between stationary and rotating parts will be limited to that required for the safe operation of the machine. Also if cutter blocks are fitted which have helical blades, the smooth transition of the curved cutting edge next to the stationary table instead of the abrupt impact of a normal blade will reduce the noise considerably.

Active noise control

191 Active noise control is an electronic-controlled noise reduction method and involves the reduction or cancellation of one sound by the introduction of a second sound having equal amplitude, but with reversed phase (see Figure 22). The second sound is usually derived electronically from the original, with the aid of a microphone signal processing system and loudspeaker. Designing and commissioning these systems must be carried out by people experienced in this field.

192 The technique can be particularly effective in reducing low-frequency noise, where control by passive measures can be difficult. It has been used

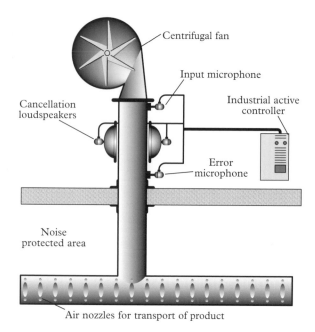

Figure 22 An active noise control system to reduce fan noise

to control noise in ducted systems such as diesel engine exhausts and the low-frequency rumble from gas turbine stacks. It has also been used to extend the performance of ear protection and noise-reducing helmets.

Maintenance

193 Machine maintenance can be very effective in limiting noise emission. Machines deteriorate with age and use and maintenance can, if carried out periodically, limit the increased noise emission due to wear.

Modification of the routes by which noise reaches workplaces

194 The path between the points at which noise is generated and the workplace can sometimes be modified. Some of the measures which should be considered are listed in paragraphs 195-202.

Enclosure

195 Enclosure involves placing a sound-proof cover over the noise source. Noisy machines can be enclosed fully, or a partial enclosure or an acoustic cover can be placed around a noisy part of a machine. Figure 23 outlines the features required of a typical machine enclosure.

Screens and barriers

196 This involves placing a physical obstacle between the noise source and the employees. The path between the points at which noise is generated and the workplace/receiver point can sometimes be modified by the use of an enclosure or by using

screens or barriers. These measures have limitations on the noise reduction achievable. However, to maximise their performance, consider using the methods described in paragraphs 197-200.

Sound absorbing material

197 Use sound absorbing material to control reflections within workrooms. Near to the source most sound is received by direct radiation from the machine, but further away the noise received by the direct path and that received by the reflected paths are approximately equal (see Figure 24). Absorbing material, fitted at a distance from the noise source (eg ceiling treatment) usually has little effect on the sound pressure level close to the source, but does reduce sound pressure levels further away (about 5 m in a typical factory). Treatment is more effective when the reflecting surface is close to the noise source, for example if a machine stands against a wall it might be worthwhile applying sound-absorbing material to the wall area behind the machine.

198 Absorbing material can also be useful for treating reflecting surfaces close to a person, for example when a worker sits against a reflecting wall. Even where sound absorbing material will not produce a significant reduction in sound pressure level it can sometimes provide a psychological benefit by reducing the high frequencies more than the low ones, and by suppressing reverberant sound, which is more unpleasant than sound radiated directly from machines.

Walls or screens

199 Walls or screens can be placed between the source of the noise and a receiver to stop the direct sound (and to a lesser degree the reflected sound) from reaching the receiver. Such barriers or screens should be constructed from a dense material (ie brick or sheet steel) to interrupt the noise transmission path. The maximum performance of a screen will only be achieved when the area in which it is located has little or no reflective sound.

200 Covering the barrier or screen with absorbent material on the side facing the noise source will have the added advantage of reducing the sound reflected back into that area containing the noise source (see paragraph 197). Those workplaces which have already been treated with sound absorbing material will help to create acoustic conditions which will allow the screen or barrier to perform to its maximum potential.

Noise refuges

201 The employee workstation itself can be 'enclosed' by providing a cabin or 'noise refuge',

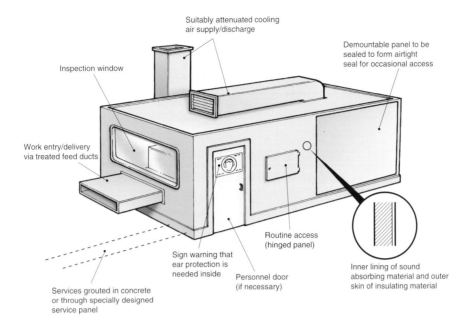

Figure 23 Example of machine enclosure

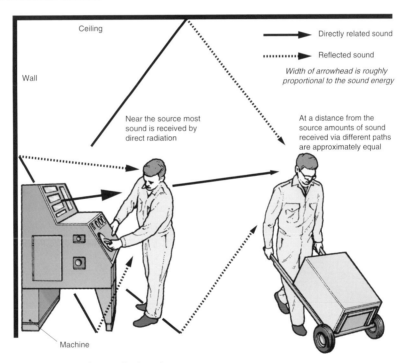

Figure 24 Paths by which airborne noise reached work areas

which is an acoustically designed enclosure (with proper regard for its ventilation and seating arrangements). If controls are brought into the cabin it will be possible to reduce the need to enter noisy areas. Even where the worker still needs to use ear protectors outside the noise refuge it can help by providing relief from the need to wear the protectors continually.

Distance

202 Increasing the distance between a person and the noise source can provide considerable noise reductions to the receiver. Some ways of achieving this are:

• to place the discharge from exhausts well away from workers. For example, pneumatically powered equipment can often be fitted with a flexible exhaust hose discharging several metres away from the operator. Similarly, on a mobile machine powered by an internal combustion engine the exhaust can be kept well away from the driving position;

• to use remote control, or automated

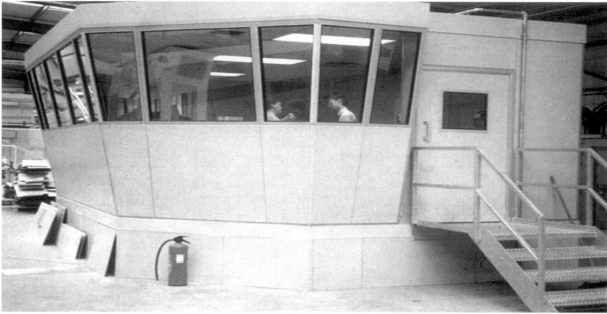

Figure 25 A noise refuge for employees

equipment to avoid the need for workers to spend long periods near to machines;

- to separate noisy processes to restrict the number of people exposed to high levels of noise, for example engine testing in test cells which need to be entered only occasionally; arrangements for quiet inspection tasks to be carried out away from noisy manufacturing areas; and location of unattended air compressors and refrigeration plant etc in separate rooms.

Reduction of exposure times

Job design

203 Noisy devices should only be used when they are actually needed. For example the pneumatic ejector on a power press need be on only for the short time required to eject the product; the air supply should be 'pulsed' to operate only when the product needs removing.

Job rotation

204 In any workplace where all the workers are trained to operate all the machines, moving them around between noisy and quiet machines for short periods during the day will reduce the overall noise exposure of all the workforce. This will prevent one operator being exposed to high noise levels on their own throughout the day.

Information and training on noise control

205 Application of noise control technology can often be difficult, with the potential to misdirect effort, time and money. Therefore noise control should be designed by someone with the knowledge and skill to understand the techniques available and assess the benefits they can bring. Where engineers need additional training, some technical colleges offer suitable courses in noise control engineering (see also Part 3 of this book).

206 However, if the measures are to be efficient it will also be necessary to take into account the operational requirements, so the engineers will also need to understand the process or collaborate with others who do. There will also be situations where a working knowledge of the process involved and alternative ways of doing the job are more important than specialised acoustical training, for example where a noisy process can be replaced by a quieter one. Some development work is in any case likely to be needed to identify and overcome problems encountered when introducing new ways of controlling noise.

Part 6

Selection and use of personal ear protection - Advice for employers

Overview

Selection

- What types of ear protection are available and which are the most suitable?

- Will the ear protection selected reduce noise exposure to below the action level?

- Will it do this without making users feel isolated or preventing them from hearing audible warnings?

- Is the ear protection suitable for the working environment?

- Is the ear protection compatible with other safety equipment?

Use

- When should ear protection be worn?

- How should ear protectors be fitted and worn?

- How should ear protectors be maintained?

Introduction

207 The use of ear protection is a last resort to control noise exposure. It should only be considered where it is not reasonably practicable to control exposure by other means.

208 Part 6 provides you with detailed advice on the types of protector that are available and how you should select and use them. You may find it helpful to involve your employee or safety representative(s). Further information on the selection, use, care and maintenance of ear protection can be found in British Standard BS EN 458: 1994 *Hearing protectors - Recommendations for selection, use, care and maintenance - Guidance document.*

Types of protector

209 Ear protectors are available in many forms. They are all capable of providing a reduction in noise exposure and all will be provided with information to allow you to decide whether they provide adequate noise reduction for your work

situation. Whichever type of protector is used, it will only provide the assumed protection if it is in good condition, is the correct size and is worn properly. The headsets supplied with personal stereos provide little or no attenuation of external noise.

210 All ear protection should carry CE marking, an indication that it meets a set of essential safety requirements, in accordance with the Personal Protective Equipment (EC Directive) Regulations 1992.

211 The three principal ear protection types are muffs, plugs and semi-inserts. There are similar ranges in noise reduction performance offered by these different types, though each will offer some advantages in certain applications. Your choice is likely to be based on factors such as:

- the predicted noise reduction;

- compatibility with other safety equipment;

- the need for communication;

- environmental factors, such as temperature or the presence of dust in the atmosphere;

- the cost of maintenance or replacement;

- comfort; and

- personal preference.

Issuing ear protection

212 When issuing ear protectors you will need to consider regulations 9, 10 and 11 of the Noise Regulations (see Part 1) and take account of the points in paragraphs 213-222.

Information

213 You should provide your employees with information on:

- why you are issuing ear protectors;

- where employees should use them;

- how they can obtain replacements or new protectors; and

- how they should wear them properly and look after them (regulations 9 and 10).

Ready availability

214 You should ensure that employees can readily obtain ear protectors and replacements when they need them. This might include personal issue to

individual employees. Alternatively, you might wish to install dispensers from which employees can take disposable ear protectors as they need them. Locate the dispensers outside the ear protection zone, in a place where your employees can conveniently use them, and you must keep them topped up.

Comfort and personal choice

215 Individuals differ in what they find comfortable. Some people prefer earplugs in hot environments, but others find any earplug extremely uncomfortable and prefer muffs. Wherever possible you should make more than one type of protector available (making sure that each is suitable for the noise and the jobs to be done) to allow the user a personal choice.

216 All protectors are likely to be somewhat uncomfortable, especially in hot, humid conditions. Therefore, choose ear protection which is sufficient to control the risk, but does not over protect and is reasonably comfortable to wear.

Personal issue and visitors

217 People should not pass earplugs to one another. Preferably, a set of earmuffs should be used by one individual only. Where earmuffs are kept for the use of visitors, they should be hygienically cleaned for each new wearer. Alternatively, disposable covers may be used.

Training and effective use

218 Ear protection will only provide good protection when used properly and it should be fitted by someone who has received appropriate training. Users must be instructed in its correct fitting and use, including:

- how to avoid potential interference on the effectiveness of their ear protection of long hair, spectacles, earrings etc;

- how to wear their ear protection in combination with other personal protection;

- the importance of wearing their ear protection at all times in a noisy environment (removing it for only a few minutes in a shift will lower the protection to the wearer considerably);

- how to store their ear protection correctly;

- how to care for and to check their ear protection at frequent intervals;

- where to report damage to their ear protection.

219 This training may be provided by the competent person, or a suitably trained supervisor.

220 Some people tend to remove ear protectors when speaking to others in noisy environments. You should advise users not to do this and explain to them that once they are used to the situation they will be able to communicate more easily with protectors than without them.

221 Some people tend to speak quietly when they are wearing ear protectors in noisy areas because they can hear their own voice more clearly. This can cause communication problems, so you should advise users to speak up when wearing protectors.

Care and maintenance

222 Ear protection must be monitored for wear and damage and replaced when necessary. If ear protectors are to be effective, and provide the expected protection, they must be in good condition. You are responsible for ensuring that ear protection is well maintained; employees are responsible for reporting any defects (see regulation 10). With experience, simple checks can be made by visual inspection and feel. It is good practice to keep a set of new protectors on display, to provide a basis for comparison.

Earmuffs

223 These are normally hard plastic cups which fit over and surround the ears, and are sealed to the head by cushion seals filled with a soft plastic foam or a viscous liquid. The inner surfaces of the cups are covered with a sound absorbing material, usually a soft plastic foam. The user should ensure that they completely surround the ear, and that there are no gaps in the contact between the cushion seal and the head.

224 Various kinds of headband are used to hold and press the muffs to the head though none are ideal for all conditions. A band over the top of the head is comfortable and allows the muffs to be slipped off when not needed, but prevents use of a hat or helmet. It is easier to wear hats or helmets with earmuffs if the headband runs behind the wearer's neck or under the chin with the muffs supported by a thin strap under the hat. Other types of earmuff are attached to safety helmets and can be swung out of the way when not needed. Headbands must be treated with care - avoid over-bending or twisting which may degrade the acoustic performance of the earmuff.

225 Where earmuffs are attached to safety head-gear such as a visor or a helmet the performance of the earmuff will be different from the equivalent

Figure 26   Muff-type ear protectors

muff on a standard headband. It is important that noise attenuation data is obtained for the specific combination of earmuffs and helmet.

Communication equipment

226   Communication equipment can be built into earmuffs, receiving signals from a wired or aerial system. In some situations, however, such communication devices may reduce overall safety. Some of the safety points to watch for are:

- the sound level reproduced by the communication system should not itself be a new noise hazard;

- where the muffs are used to receive spoken messages the microphone should, where possible, be switched off when not in use, to avoid the reproduction inside the muff of spurious background noise;

- checks should be made to ensure it is possible to hear necessary warning sounds (eg speech)* above the sounds reproduced under the muff;

- safety alarms should not normally be relayed through the communication system because of the risk of system failure.

* Standard methods are available for selecting suitable auditory warning signals - ISO 7731: 1986 *Danger signals for workplaces - Auditory danger signals.*

Care and maintenance of earmuffs

227   It is essential that earmuffs are regularly checked and maintained. Points to remember include:

- Check the cup seals for general cleanliness and for signs of hardening, tearing and deformation. Service kits, including new seals, are available from most manufacturers.

- Check the cup condition for cracks, holes and unofficial modifications.

- Check the tension in the headband. This can be carried out by holding the headband at its mid-point on the end of a finger; if there is a gap between the cups, the headband tension may have reduced. Check by comparison with a new muff.

- Check the seals on helmet-mounted muffs. If they sit on the side of a helmet for long periods they will become deformed.

- If users notice any skin irritation around the area of the head where the seal fits, they must seek medical advice immediately and also inform their supervisor.

- Earmuffs must be stored in a clean environment and cleaned following the manufacturers' instructions.

Comfort

228 One of the factors affecting the comfort of earmuffs is the pressure of the seals on the head. This can be kept low by using resilient seals which only need a low headband force. A high contact area between seal and head also helps reduce the contact pressure, but in hot conditions can cause the skin to sweat.* Other important factors affecting comfort include the weight of the muffs (the lighter the better) and the size of the muff cup (the cups must be large enough to fit right over the user's ears).

Effective use of earmuffs

229 Muff-type ear protectors are easy to use and are clearly visible, so the wearing of ear protection can be easily monitored. However, they are not suited to use with safety glasses or some types of helmet and may be uncomfortable in warm environments. Helmets and face shields might prevent earmuffs fitting correctly if there is insufficient clearance between them and the muffs. Where ear-protection has to be worn inside a helmet, the user's ability to move their head comfortably will need to be checked.

*Liners which fit between the seal and the head can absorb sweat, but may reduce protection by a small amount (typically 2 to 4 dB(A)).

230 There should be no interference with earmuff seals. As illustrated in Figure 28, anything between the seal and head is likely to reduce performance. Goggles and spectacles should have thin frames, or should be held by straps which do not pass under the seal. Beards, long hair and clothing such as scarves worn under the seals can also reduce the performance of muffs.

Earplugs

231 Earplugs fit into the ear canal. They sometimes have a cord or neckband to prevent loss. Some earplugs are intended to be used for an indefinite time (permanent), others to be used a few times (reusable) and some to be thrown away after one use (disposable).

232 Before you first issue earplugs you should ask the user whether he or she has any ear trouble such as irritation of the ear canal, earache, discharge of the ears, or is under treatment for any ear disease. You should refer people who report such troubles to a doctor for an opinion on whether they may use the devices with safety.

Figure 27 Helmet-mounted, muff-type ear protectors

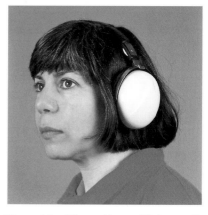
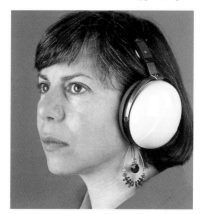

Figure 28 The problems of fitting muff-type ear protectors (eg with long hair, safety glasses or jewellery)

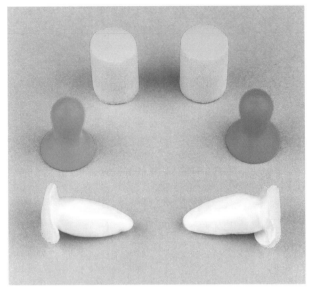

Figure 29 Plug-type ear protectors

Disposable and 'reusable' plugs

233 These are convenient to issue and are probably the most widely used type of earplug. They are made from various compressible materials such as plastic foam or fine mineral down (often contained in a plastic membrane) and can be used by most people without requiring specialist fitting.

'Permanent' rubber or plastic plugs

234 These are usually available in a range of sizes. To obtain a good seal in the ear canal it is essential that the correct size is used, resulting in a slightly tight fit. Some people may need a different size plug for each ear.

Custom-moulded plugs

235 Custom-moulded earplugs are made from a material such as silicone rubber, individually moulded to fit a person's ears. They must be made by someone properly trained in the process, can give good results and are comfortable. An advantage of this type of plug over standard earplugs is that it is easier to fit the plugs correctly, therefore the user is more likely to get the predicted protection.

Care and maintenance of earplugs

236 It is essential that earplugs are regularly checked and maintained. Points to remember include:

● Disposable earplugs should be used only once.

● Washable earplugs should be cleaned according to the manufacturer's instructions, and stored in a clean container until next required.

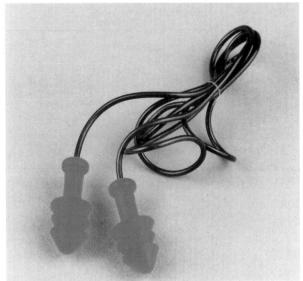

Figure 30 Earplugs with a cord attachment

● Check reusable earplugs for resilience and softness.

● Hands should be clean when fitting earplugs.

● Reusable and washable earplugs should only be on individual issue and used by one person.

● Where disposable earplugs are used, adequate supplies of new plugs must always be available.

Comfort

237 The comfort of earplugs will largely depend on the pressure on the contact area between ear canal and plug. Types which mould themselves readily to the shape of the user's ear canal and custom-moulded plugs are usually found to be the most comfortable.

Effective use of earplugs

238 Earplugs will only be effective when fitted properly so correct fitting is essential. They need to be properly and securely inserted into the ear canal if they are to make a good seal and should not work loose during use. Users must be instructed in the correct fitting of their earplugs. It is difficult for a supervisor to see whether plugs are properly inserted, so it is particularly important to make sure that the user knows how to do this.

239 Permanent and reusable plugs need to be cleaned regularly. With age the material may degrade, resulting in loss of fit and protection, so the employer's programme needs to include provision for regular replacement. The supplier should be asked for advice on suitable methods of cleaning and the life expectancy of the plugs.

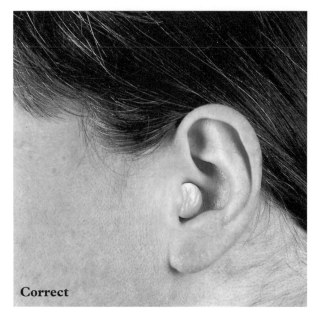
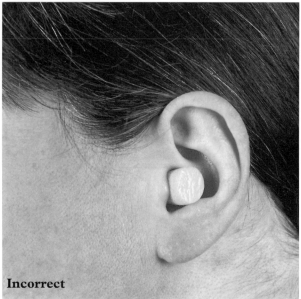

Correct

Incorrect

Figure 31 The correct and incorrect fitting of earplugs

240 Earplugs are suited to use with safety glasses or some forms of helmet. They may not be suitable where the ear protection is likely to be removed often, particularly in dusty or dirty environments.

Semi-inserts

241 These are pre-moulded ear caps attached to a headband which presses them against the entrance of the ear canal. This type of protector can be useful for those who spend short periods of time in ear protection zones.

Special types of protector

242 Sophisticated ear protectors are now available which provide additional noise control facilities, for example built-in electronic systems. You should

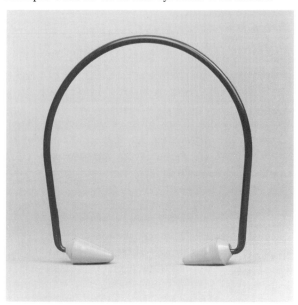

Figure 32 Semi-insert ear protectors

take care when selecting this type of protector since standard test methods are not yet available which are directly appropriate to some of them.★ Currently, manufacturers often provide noise reduction information on these specialist protectors based on their own test methods and you should ensure that they will provide adequate protection in your circumstances.

Level-dependent protectors

243 Level-dependent (or amplitude sensitive) ear protectors are designed to protect against hazardous noise while permitting good communication when it is quieter. They are most suited to situations where the noise exposure is intermittent and there is a need to communicate during quieter intervals.

244 Sound-restoration, level-dependent earmuffs are available, incorporating an electronic sound reproduction system. At low sound pressure levels, the sound detected by a microphone on the outside of the muff is relayed to a loudspeaker inside the muff cup. At high sound pressure levels, the electronic controls cut out the reproduced sound, allowing the muff to provide its full attenuation.

245 Level-dependent devices based on non-electronic methods are also available. These use the acoustic properties of carefully designed air ducts

★ In 1997 only BS EN 24869-1: 1993 *Acoustics - Sound attenuation of hearing protectors. Part 1 - Subjective method of measurement* is available which is designed for passive protector types. This test is not generally suitable for protectors with built-in electronic noise control systems. A standard is in preparation for amplitude-dependent ear protectors.

to give different attenuation properties at different noise levels. These types of protector are designed to be effective against very high single impulse noises, such as firearms, rather than the continuous noise or repetitive impulses found in most industrial situations.

Active noise reduction protectors

246 Active noise reduction (ANR) ear protectors incorporate an electronic sound cancelling system to achieve greater noise attenuation. ANR is particularly effective at low frequencies (50-500 Hz) where normal, passive earmuffs are least effective. ANR protectors are therefore usually based on a muff-type protector, to give high attenuation at all frequencies. In current (1997) devices, the ANR systems typically improve the noise reduction by around 15 dB at frequencies below 160 Hz.

Flat frequency response protectors

247 Most ear protectors provide greater attenuation at high frequencies than they do at low frequencies. In some applications, it is important to be able to hear the high-frequency sound at the correct level relative to the low-frequency sounds, for example musicians during rehearsal and practising. Ear protectors are available which are specifically designed for this type of application, giving a similar attenuation value (flat frequency response) across the whole frequency range.

Dual protection

248 Situations may arise where the sound pressure level is extremely high, so that muffs or earplugs alone are not able to provide sufficient protection. This problem is likely where the daily noise exposure is above 115 dB(A) or the peak sound pressure level exceeds 160 dB, especially if there is substantial noise at frequencies less than about 500 Hz.

249 Improved protection can be obtained by wearing a combination of earmuffs and earplugs. The amount of protection will depend on the particular muff and plug combination. In general, the most useful combination is a high-performance plug with a moderate-performance earmuff (a high-performance earmuff adds a little extra protection but is likely to be less comfortable).

250 If dual protection is used, test data should be obtained for the particular combination of plug and muff (and helmet, if used). It cannot be assumed that the protection will be equal to the sum of the assumed protection value (APV) of the individual plug and muff (see Figure 33). In practice, the increase in APV you can expect from dual protection will be no more than 6 dB(A) over the APV of the better of the individual protectors.

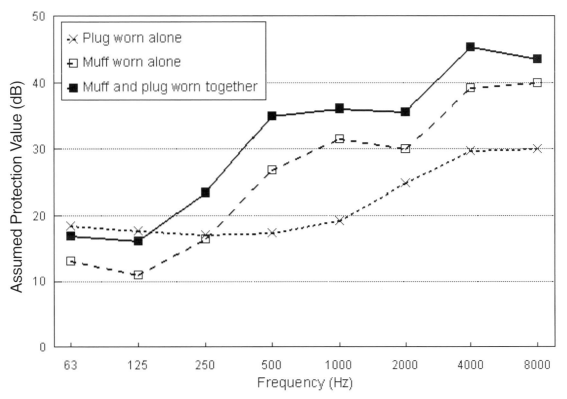

Figure 33 Assumed protection values for a separate earmuff and earplug and for the same muff and plug worn together

Maximising performance of protectors

251 Manufacturers provide information on the noise reduction which can be expected from their ear protectors. This information is obtained from a standard test, defined in British Standard BS EN 24869-1: 1993* (see Appendix 6). This test assumes that the protectors will be well fitted and are properly used. In practice, there are many reasons why ear protectors give less attenuation than that predicted by the manufacturer's data, some of the more common are:

- earmuffs incompatible with other equipment worn (see paragraphs 224-225);

- interference with earmuff seals (see paragraph 230);

- incorrect fitting of earplugs (see paragraph 238);

- 'real-world' attenuation. In practical work situations, research has shown that the attenuation provided by earmuffs, when used in the work environment, is about 5 dB less than predicted by manufacturers' average attenuation data. For earplugs, a greater variability is found, with difference up to 18 dB observed. This increased variation is principally due to the poor fitting of plugs;

- failure to use protectors all of the time in noisy areas. If the protectors are removed in noisy areas, even for short periods, the amount of protection provided will be severely limited. For example, if a protector with a predicted noise level reduction (PNR) of 30 dB(A) is removed for 15 minutes in an 8-hour working day, the actual reduction in personal noise exposure will be 15 dB(A). Table 2 and Figure 34 show the protection actually achieved, if protectors are worn for less than all of an 8-hour shift.

252 The example in Figure 34 is for a person working in a continuous noise level of 113 dB(A) who has been supplied with ear protection capable of 30 dB(A) noise reduction. If this protection was worn throughout the full 8-hour working day, the person's resulting exposure ($L_{EP,d}$) would be 83 dB(A). The line shows the drastic effect on the exposure if the ear protection is worn for periods of less than 8 hours while still in the same noise.

* This standard superseded a previous British Standard BS 5108 and is equivalent to International Standard ISO 4869-1: 1990.

Table 2   Change in predicted noise exposure if ear protection is not worn all of the time (this example is based on an ear protector capable of 30 dB(A) reduction in the 113 dB(A) continuous sound pressure level).

Percentage of time protector is worn	Time worn during an 8-hour day	Actual noise reduction (dB(A))
0%	Not worn	–
50%	4 hours	3
75%	6 hours	6
87%	7 hours	9
94%	7 hours 30 minutes	12
97%	7 hours 45 minutes	15
97.9%	7 hours 50 minutes	16.6
99%	7 hours 55 minutes	18.5
99.6%	7 hours 58 minutes	23
99.82%	7 hours 59 minutes	25.5
100%	All day (8 hours)	30

Estimate the noise reduction provided by ear protectors

253 When you select ear protectors, you must estimate the noise exposure with the ear protection worn to assess whether it is below the required action level. The estimate will be based on the standardised information provided by the ear protection manufacturers (see Appendix 6). The methods used for estimating reduction in $L_{EP,d}$ and reduction in peak sound pressure level are different.

254 For the reduction in $L_{EP,d}$, you must estimate the 'effective A-weighted sound pressure level', L'_A which is determined from:

- the sound pressure level;

- information on the frequency content of the noise; and

- information on the noise reduction performance of the ear protector.

255 Appendix 6 gives details of the methods which can be used to estimate L'_A.

256 For impulsive noise, where the protectors must reduce the peak sound pressure level to below the peak action level, the noise reduction can often be estimated using the method given in Appendices 11 and 12, using:

- the peak sound pressure level; and

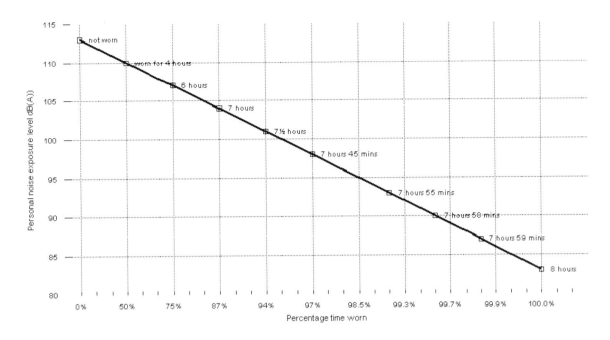

Figure 34 The effect of wearing time on the performance of ear protection

• information on the noise reduction performance of the ear protector.

257 However, this method can not be applied to noise with significant low-frequency content. In such cases specialised noise measurements must be made.

258 Sound pressure level information will be available from your noise assessment. Frequency content information may be in the form of a frequency spectrum or a simple measurement of the C-weighted sound pressure level. The noise reduction information is obtained from information provided by the ear protector manufacturers.

259 The protectors should be chosen so that:

• L_A' is below the second action level (it is good practice to choose the protectors so that L_A' is below the first action level) or the peak SPL is below the peak action level;

• L_A' is not less than 75 dB, to avoid over-protection which tends to make the wearer feel isolated;

• the overall noise exposure is reduced by at least 5 dB(A), to avoid the use of protectors of little real value.

260 For workers with variable exposures, you should make sure that your employees have protectors adequate for the worst situation likely to be encountered and that they know when and where to use them.

Appendix 1　Standards for the performance and periodic testing of sound level meters, dosemeters and sound calibrators

Performance

1　The performance of noise measurement instrumentation is specified by International, European and British standards. The current standards are included in Table A1. All the standards listed for each type of equipment are identical but published under different numbers through different standards organisations. Numbers under which identical standards have been previously published in the UK are listed as old British Standards.

2　Instruments used for assessments should meet the requirements of current standards. If you have instruments which predate these standards, ask the manufacturer to confirm whether the instrument can meet current standards. Instrument standards are subject to review and change, so when you buy new instruments for assessments, you should ensure that they comply with the latest standards.

3　Sound level meters and sound calibrators are specified to different grades of accuracy as given in Table A1. Note that Type 3 sound level meters (integrating and non-integrating) are not suitable for noise assessments.

Periodic testing

4　The meters and sound calibrators used for assessments must be retested at least every two years to verify they still meet the standards, and also retested after any repair likely to affect the performance. BS 7580: 1997 (Parts 1 and 2) gives periodic verification tests for sound level meters, while tests for dosemeters are included in the dosemeter standards in Table A1. (At the time of writing, the draft for IEC 61672 also includes procedures for periodic verification.) Testing should ideally be carried out by a laboratory with suitable accreditation.

Table A1 Current standards and old British Standards specifying integrating and non-integrating sound level meters, personal sound exposure meters (dosemeters) and sound calibrators

Equipment type	Grades	Current standards	Old British Standards
Sound level meter	Type 0 (laboratory reference) Type 1 (laboratory and field) Type 2 (general field) Type 3 (field check)	EN 60651: 1994[*] BS EN 60651: 1994[*] IEC 651: 1979[*]	BS 5969: 1981
Integrating sound level meter	Type 0 (laboratory reference) Type 1 (laboratory and field) Type 2 (general field) Type 3 (field check)	EN 60804: 1994[*] BS EN 60804: 1994[*] IEC 804: 1985[*]	BS 6698: 1986
Personal sound exposure meter (dosemeter)	Single grade only	EN 61252: 1995 BS EN 61252: 1997 IEC 1252: 1993	BS 6402: 1994
Sound calibrator	Class 0 (most accurate) Class 1 Class 2 (least accurate)	BS 7189: 1989 IEC 942: 1988	None

[*] At the time of writing, the standards for sound level meters and integrating sound level meters are being revised into a proposed combined standard, to be published as IEC 61672. Two grades are specified (Class 1 and 2) which will be approximately equivalent to Types 1 and 2 in accuracy but with some additional and increased performance requirements.

Appendix 2   Measurement of noise very close to the ear

1   When a person is receiving significant noise exposure from sources close to the ear such as communication headsets or earpieces, or they are wearing helmets which cover the ear (such as shot-blasting, or motorcycle helmets) very different methods are required to measure their noise exposure than those described in Part 4. Note that these measurements are complex and should only be carried out by those with the necessary expertise.

Use of miniature microphones

2   Miniature microphones on the ear or at the entrance to the ear canal can be used, provided the sound source is itself not inserted into the ear (such as with some types of earpiece) or the microphone does not contact directly with the sound source.

3   Close to the ear, the sound field and the sound levels at different frequencies are altered by the ear. Corrections must therefore be applied before the measurement can be used to give the person's noise exposure. This correction requires analysing the sound into bands, no wider than a third octave, and applying a different correction to each frequency band before summing the levels to obtain the equivalent A-weighted level without the disturbance of the head and ear. The correction required will depend on the position and frequency response of the miniature microphone.

4   A method of obtaining a correction is to record the spectrum and level of a diffuse sound field of random noise with a miniature microphone in position in the person's ear and to repeat the measurement with a high quality microphone in the same position in the sound field but without the person present. The difference between the two measurements will give the correction for each frequency band measured with the miniature microphone. At some frequencies and some positions of the miniature microphone, the corrections may vary from person to person, and several measurements on different people may be required to obtain a representative average correction.

Use of a HATS

5   An alternative to measuring at the human ear is to use a HATS (head and torso simulator) which has a realistic simulated ear (pinna, ear canal and eardrum). A HATS can also be used for measuring the noise from insert ear pieces (in communication systems), since the measurement of the sound pressure level is made at the simulated eardrum; such measurements are extremely difficult using human subjects.

6   HATS are most suited to laboratory measurements and passive listening, rather than assessing noise exposure arising from work activities (such as shot-blasting). Also a HATS may not be suitable for measurements on headsets which seal around the ear (circumaural types).

7   When using a HATS, a similar correction to that described for miniature microphones is required to correct the level measured in the ear. The HATS manufacturer should be able to supply this correction for you.

Standards

8   There are no standards for the methods described above, and only a limited standard for HATS (IEC 959). However, an international standard is being prepared for determining noise exposure levels due to sound sources close to the ears.*

---

* Draft ISO 11904 Parts 1 and 2

Appendix 3   Calculation of $L_{EP,d}$ from sound pressure level measurements

Nomogram method (see Figure 3 in Part 4)

1   Where a person receives all their significant noise exposure at just one level, the $L_{EP,d}$ can be read from the nomogram centre scale where a line between the level (measured either as the A-weighted SPL or A-weighted L_{eq}) on the left-hand scale and the exposure duration on the right-hand scale intersects.

Step 1   Draw a straight line connecting the measured level on the left-hand scale with the exposure duration on the right-hand scale.

Step 2   Where the line intersects the centre scale read the $L_{EP,d}$.

Example 1

A person works at a noisy machine for 2 hours 15 minutes each day. The measured A-weighted L_{eq} where they work is 102 dB(A). The remainder of the day is spent in a quiet office where the level is below 70 dB(A), which is sufficiently low to be ignored.

Step 1   Draw a straight line connecting the level of 102 dB(A) on the left-hand scale with the exposure duration of 2 hours 15 minutes on the right-hand scale.

Step 2   The line intersects the centre scale at a $L_{EP,d}$ of 97 dB(A) (rounded up to the whole decibel).

2   When the daily exposure is made up of periods at different levels, each measured separately, the fractional exposure value for each period is read from the nomogram. The $L_{EP,d}$ is read from the nomogram centre scale at the point corresponding to the sum of the daily fractional exposure values.

Step 1   For each noise exposure draw a straight line connecting the level on the left-hand scale with the corresponding exposure duration on the right-hand scale.

Step 2   Where the line intersects the centre scale read the fractional exposure value.

Step 3   Sum the fractional exposure values from each noise exposure.

Step 4   Read the $L_{EP,d}$ from the centre scale adjacent to the summed fractional exposure value.

Example 2

During a 12-hour shift, a person is exposed at the following levels for the periods shown during a working day. The fractional exposure values correspond to the intersection of the line, connecting the level and duration of each exposure, on the nomogram centre scale (Steps 1 and 2).

Sound level dB(A)	Duration of exposure	Fractional exposure value from nomogram
102	15 minutes	0.5
90	50 minutes	0.1
83	10 hours	0.25
less than 80	55 minutes	-

To determine the $L_{EP,d}$:

Step 3   Sum the fractional exposure values for each noise exposure: 0.85

Step 4   Read the corresponding $L_{EP,d}$ from the centre scale: 90 dB(A) (rounded up to the whole decibel).

Calculator method

3   Where a person receives all their significant noise exposure at one level during the day the $L_{EP,d}$ can be calculated as shown:

Step 1   Divide the measured sound level, L, by 10 $L/10$

Step 2   Convert to the antilog $10^{L/10}$

Step 3   Multiply by the duration t in hours $t.10^{L/10}$

Step 4   Divide by 8 $\dfrac{t.10^{L/10}}{8}$

Step 5   Convert to the log $\log\dfrac{t.10^{L/10}}{8}$

Step 6   Multiply by 10 $10\log\dfrac{t.10^{L/10}}{8}$

4   Where the exposure is made up of separate exposures at different levels, proceed through Steps 1, 2 and 3 for each level and duration of exposure. Sum the resultant values in the calculator memory as shown below.

$$t_1.10^{L_1/10} + t_2.10^{L_2/10} + ...t_n.10^{L_n/10}$$

Using the summed value proceed through Steps 4, 5 and 6.

5   Examples 3 and 4 use the calculator method to repeat the $L_{EP,d}$ evaluation of Examples 1 and 2.

Example 3

A person works at a noisy machine for 2 hours 15 minutes each day. The measured A-weighted L_{eq} at their workstation is 102 dB(A). The remainder of the day is spent in a quiet office where the level is below 70 dB(A), which is sufficiently low to be ignored.

Step 1	Divide the measured sound level L by 10	10.2
Step 2	Convert to the antilog	1.58×10^{10}
Step 3	Multiply by the duration t in hours	3.57×10^{10}
Step 4	Divide by 8	4.46×10^9
Step 5	Convert to the log	9.65
Step 6	Multiply by 10	$L_{EP,d}$ = **97 dB(A)**

(rounded up to the whole decibel)

Example 4

A person is exposed at the following levels for the periods shown during a working day. For each separate exposure use Steps 1, 2 and 3 to obtain the $t.10^{L/10}$ value.

Sound level dB(A)	Duration of exposure	$t.10^{L/10}$ value
102	15 minutes	3.96×10^9
90	50 minutes	8.33×10^8
83	10 hours	2.0×10^9

Step 4a	Sum $t.10^{L/10}$ values	6.79×10^9
Step 4	Divide by 8	8.49×10^8
Step 5	Convert to the log	8.93
Step 6	Multiply by 10	$L_{EP,d}$ = **90 dB(A)**

(rounded up to the whole decibel)

Appendix 4 Calculation of $L_{EP,d}$ from dosemeter measurements

Nomogram method (see Figure 3 in Part 4)

1   If the measurement period covers only part of the working day, but is representative of the exposure during the rest of the day, calculate the daily dose as shown:

Step 1   Daily dose = $\dfrac{\text{Measured dose x Exposure duration}}{\text{Measurement time}}$

Step 2   **If the dose is given in Pa².h** divide the daily dose by 3.2 to obtain the equivalent fractional noise exposure, f, and read the corresponding $L_{EP,d}$ from the centre scale of the nomogram.

$$f = \frac{\text{Dose (in Pa}^2\text{.h)}}{3.2}$$

If the dose is given as a percentage divide the daily dose by 100 to obtain the fractional exposure, and read the corresponding $L_{EP,d}$ from the centre scale of the nomogram.

$$f = \frac{\text{percentage dose}}{100}$$

Example 5

A dosemeter worn for an entire 9-hour shift gives a reading of 4.8 Pa².h.

Step 1   Daily dose equals measured dose since the measurement time covers the full exposure duration.

Step 2   The fractional exposure value:
4.8/3.2 = 1.5
On the centre scale of the nomogram this corresponds to an $L_{EP,d}$ of **92 dB(A)**

2   On some dosemeters, the 100% dose is not equivalent to an $L_{EP,d}$ of 90 dB(A) (see Example 6). In these cases an additional step is required:

Step 3   Correct the $L_{EP,d}$ from the nomogram (to allow for the difference between 90 dB(A) and the $L_{EP,d}$ corresponding to 100% on the dosemeter).

Correct $L_{EP,d} = L_{EP,d \text{ (nomogram)}} + L_{EP,d(100\%)} - 90$ dB(A)

Example 6

A dosemeter is worn for 2.5 hours between breaks and the recorded noise dose is 57% where 100% on the dosemeter is equivalent to an $L_{EP,d}$ of 85 dB(A). The total time at work is 8.5 hours including 1.5 hours of breaks in a quiet place (< 75 dB(A)).

The total duration of the noise exposure is 7 hours (8.5 hours minus 1.5 hours break).

Step 1   Daily dose = 57 x 7/2.5 = 160%

Step 2   Fractional exposure value
= 160/100 = 1.6.
for which the nomogram gives an $L_{EP,d}$ of 92 dB(A).

Step 3   Correct for $L_{100\%}$:
$L_{EP,d}$ = 92 + 85 - 90 = **87 dB(A)**

Calculator method

3   If the measurement period covers only part of the working day, but is representative of the exposure during the rest of the day, calculate the daily dose as shown.

For a dose in Pa².h

Step 1	Daily dose = $\dfrac{\text{Measured dose x Exposure duration}}{\text{Measurement time}}$	
Step 2	Divide the daily dose by 3.2	daily dose/3.2
Step 3	Take the log	log (daily dose/3.2)
Step 4	Multiply by 10	10 log (daily dose/3.2)
Step 5	Add 90	90 + 10 log (daily dose/3.2)

For a dose as a percentage

Step 1	Daily dose = $\dfrac{\text{Measured dose x Exposure duration}}{\text{Measurement time}}$	
Step 2	Divide the daily dose by 100	daily dose /100
Step 3	Take the log	log (daily dose/100)
Step 4	Multiply by 10	10 log (daily dose/100)
Step 5	Add the dosemeter $L_{100\%}$ value	$L_{100\%}$ + 10 log (daily dose/100)

4   Examples 7 and 8 use the calculator method to repeat the $L_{EP,d}$ evaluation of Examples 5 and 6.

Example 7

A dosemeter worn for an entire 9-hour shift gives a reading of 4.8 $Pa^2.h$.

Step 1	The daily dose equals the measured dose since the measurement time covers the full exposure duration.	
Step 2	Divide the daily dose by 3.2	1.5
Step 3	Take the log	0.18
Step 4	Multiply by 10	1.8
Step 5	Add 90	91.8

$L_{EP,d} =$ **92 dB(A)** (rounded up to the whole decibel).

Example 8

A dosemeter is worn for 2.5 hours between breaks and the recorded noise dose is 57% where 100% on the dosemeter is equivalent to an $L_{EP,d}$ of 85 dB(A). The total time at work is 8.5 hours including 1.5 hours break time in a quiet place (<75 dB(A)).

The total duration of the noise exposure is 7 hours (8.5 hours minus 1.5 hours break).

Step 1	Daily dose	57 x 7/2.5 = 160%
Step 2	Divide the daily dose by 100	160/100 = 1.6
Step 3	Take the log	log 1.6 = 0.20
Step 4	Multiply by 10	10 x 0.20 = 2.0
Step 5	Add the dosemeter $L_{100\%}$ value (in this case 85 dB)	85 + 2 = 87

$L_{EP,d} =$ **87 dB(A)**

Appendix 5   Calculation of $L_{EP,d}$ from short-duration noise using sound exposure level (SEL) measurements

Nomogram method

1   The nomogram in Figure 4 (in Part 4) can be used to convert from an SEL measurement to the $L_{EP,d}$ or fractional exposure value.

Step 1   Divide the number of events in a day (n) by the number of events in the period of the SEL measurement (m) to give the ratio: n/m.

Step 2   Draw a line connecting the measured SEL on the left-hand scale to the value of n/m on the right-hand scale. Read the fractional exposure value at the intersection on the centre scale.

Step 3   Add all the fractional exposures for the day's work (include the fractional exposure for the background noise) taken from the nomograms in Figures 3 and 4 (in Part 4).

Step 4   From the centre scale on either nomogram read the $L_{EP,d}$ corresponding to the sum of the fractional exposure values.

Example 9

Proof firings are carried out of five shot gun cartridges. The peak SPL is measured at 135 dB, ie below the 140 dB peak action level. The SEL is 123 dB(A). The operator would fire 20 cartridges per day. The background noise is below 70 dB(A). Other noise exposure during the day comes from 50 minutes spent where the level is 97 dB(A).

Step 1   Ratio, n/m   20/5 = 4

Step 2   f value from nomogram   0.27

Step 3   f value from other noise   0.5 (using Figure 3)

  Sum of f values   0.77

Step 4 $L_{EP,d}$ from nomogram   **89 dB(A)** (rounded up to the whole decibel).

Calculator method

Step 1   Divide the number of events a day by the number of events measured
$$\frac{n}{m}$$

Step 2   Convert to the log $\log\frac{n}{m}$

Step 3   Multiply by 10 $10\log\frac{n}{m}$

Step 4   Add the SEL $10\log\frac{n}{m} + SEL$

Step 5   Subtract 44.6 dB to give the $L_{EP,d}$ $10\log\frac{n}{m} + SEL - 44.6$

Step 6   Add the contribution of any other noise exposure (including any significant background noise) by summing the associated $L_{EP,d}$ for each

Overall $L_{EP,d} = 10\log(10^{L_{EP,d(1)}/10} + 10^{L_{EP,d(2)}/10} \cdots\cdots 10^{L_{EP,d(n)}/10})$

Example 10

Proof firings are carried out of five shotgun cartridges. The peak SPL is measured at 135 dB, ie below the 140 dB peak action level. The SEL is 123 dB(A). The operator would fire 20 cartridges per day. The background noise is below 70 dB(A). Other noise exposure during the day comes from 50 minutes spent where the level is 97 dB(A).

Step 1   Divide the number of events a day by the number of events measured
20/5 = 4

Step 2   Take the log   0.60

Step 3   Multiply by 10   10 x 0.60 = 6.0

Step 4   Add the measured SEL   6 + 123 = 129

Step 5   Subtract 44.6 dB to give the $L_{EP,d}$ 129 - 44.6 = 84.4

Step 6   Add the contribution of any other noise exposure

- 97 dB for 50 minutes (0.833 hours): $L_{EP,d(1)} = 10\log\frac{(0.83 \times 10^{9.7})}{8} = 87.2$

- Overall $L_{EP,d} =$ $10\log(10^{87.2/10} + 10^{84.4/10}) = 89.0$

Daily noise exposure = **89 dB(A)**

Appendix 6 Ear protection information

1   Suppliers of ear protection with CE marking are required to satisfy the relevant part of BS EN 352 which sets out basic safety requirements for ear protector features such as size, weight and durability for:

●   earmuffs (BS EN 352-1: 1993);

●   earplugs (BS EN 352-2: 1993); and

●   helmet-mounted muffs (BS EN 352-3: 1997).*

2   Ear protection which complies with BS EN 352 must be supplied with performance information derived from a standard test defined in British Standard BS ISO EN 4869-1: 1995. The information required is:

●   mean and standard deviation (std.dev) attenuation values at each octave-band centre frequency from 125 Hz to 8 kHz (63 Hz is optional);

●   assumed protection values at each centre frequency (based on mean minus one standard deviation, ie $\alpha = 1$);

●   H, M and L values in accordance with BS EN ISO 4869-2: 1994;

●   SNR value in accordance with BS EN ISO 4869-2: 1994.

* Other parts are currently (1997) in preparation for electronic, sound restoration, level-dependent muffs and for the performance of ear protectors in impulsive noise.

3   An example of the data supplied by manufacturers is shown in Table A2.

4   The BS EN 24869-1 test is a 'subjective' threshold shift procedure, in which the faintest sound audible for 16 test subjects is found. The test is repeated with and without the protectors fitted and the difference between the two sets of results is taken as a measure of the attenuation.

5   Individual measurements of attenuation will vary for a number of reasons, some of which are genuine variations in the protection different individuals will receive, due to differences in how well an ear protector fits different test subjects or slight variations in fit each time any one protector is fitted. Other variations result from the test procedure itself, such as limitations on a test subject's ability to detect consistently a 'just audible' level. For this reason the attenuation data is supplied as a mean and standard deviation.

6   The expected performance of ear protection is usually based on the assumed noise protection value, calculated as the mean minus one standard deviation. This ensures that the majority of subjects will achieve more than the predicted noise reduction. However, some subjects (16%) will receive less than the predicted noise reduction, even with new, properly fitted protectors. In some cases, it is advisable to base ear protection selection on the mean minus two standard deviations, to ensure that the majority are adequately protected, allowing for the imperfect fitting and condition of ear protectors in the working environment.

Table A2 Example of the information provided by manufacturers of ear protection (required by BS EN 352)

		Octave-band centre frequency (Hz)							
		63	125	250	500	1000	2000	4000	8000
Mean attenuation	(dB)	7.4	10.0	14.4	19.6	22.8	29.6	38.8	34.1
Standard deviation	(dB)	3.3	3.6	3.6	4.6	4.0	6.2	7.4	5.2
Assumed noise protection value (APV) = mean attenuation - std.dev	(dB)	4.1	6.4	10.8	15.0	18.8	23.4	31.4	28.9

H	M	L		SNR
25	19	13		22

7   The HML (high, medium and low) and SNR values are provided to allow simplified calculations of the effective A-weighted sound pressure levels. Like the assumed protection values, the HML and SNR values are calculated from the mean attenuation values and their standard deviations.

8   Where performance data is derived from non-standard test procedures, care is needed when interpreting the results. It is important to assess both the quality of the data and its relevance to your own work situation. Non-standard data is likely to be supplied with sound-restoration level-dependent muffs, since there is currently no standard for this type of ear protection.

Appendix 7 Methods for predicting the reduction in $L_{EP,d}$ given by ear protection

1   The sound pressure levels when ear protection is worn may be estimated using a number of different methods. The principal three methods are defined in BS EN 24869-2: 1995.*

* A fourth method, the HML check, as defined in BS EN 458: 1993, is not covered in this guidance.

Table A3 Methods of estimating sound pressure levels using BS EN 24869-2: 1995

Method	Description	Measurements required	Worked example
Octave-band	This is the most accurate prediction method, but requires the most detailed noise measurement and involves the most complicated method of calculating the effective A-weighted sound pressure level at the ear.	Octave-band spectrum	Appendix 8
HML (high, medium and low)	This is the preferred method where an octave-band spectrum is not available. Three values H, M and L are used with two simple measurements of the sound pressure level.	A-weighted and C-weighted average sound pressure levels	Appendix 9
SNR (single number rating)	The SNR value is used with a single measurement of the sound pressure level.	C-weighted average sound pressure level	Appendix 10

2   All methods will give similar predictions of noise reduction for general industrial noise. The simple methods become less accurate where the noise is dominated by noise at single frequencies, particularly where these are at low frequencies.

Octave-band method

3   The octave-band method is based on an octave-band assessment of the noise exposure (this is best done as octave-band values of the unweighted L_{eq}).

By calculation

4   To calculate the effective A-weighted sound pressure level at the ear using the octave-band method, take your octave-band noise exposure assessment, then:

Step 1   Subtract the octave-band APV data for your ear protector.

Step 2   Add the A-weighting correction factors (see Table A4) to give octave-band levels in dB(A).

Step 3   Convert to pressure equivalent levels, by dividing by 10 and taking the inverse logarithm (antilog).

Step 4   Sum the octave-band pressure equivalent levels.

Step 5   Convert this sum back to an overall dB(A) level by taking the logarithm of the sum and multiplying by 10.

Step 6   Round to the nearest whole number.

5   A worked example of this procedure is given in Appendix 8.

Table A4 A-weighting corrections (from BS EN 60651:1994)

Octave-band centre frequency Hz	63	125	250	500	1000	2000	4000	8000
A-weighting correction dB	-26.2	-16.1	-8.6	-3.2	0.0	1.2	1.0	-1.1

Graphical method*

6   This is less precise than the previous method, but is sufficiently accurate for most purposes.

Step 1   Take the octave-band noise exposure assessment and plot on the chart in Figure A2.

Step 2   Subtract the octave-band APV data for your ear protector.

Step 3   Plot the resultant octave-band sound levels on the chart illustrated in Figure A1, and the point of highest penetration into the A-weighted sound level contours should be noted. The A-weighted sound level, dB(A), is given by the contour corresponding to this point. A blank chart is included at Figure A2 for your own use.

7   In broad-band noise this graphical method is usually accurate enough for specification of ear protection. It becomes less reliable under the following conditions, neither of which arises frequently in practice:

● when the plotted sound pressure levels follow very closely an A-weighted sound level contour over more than 3 octaves. The true sound level will then be more than that indicated by the figure. It is most unlikely that the error will be more than 3 dB(A);

● when there are prominent pure tones, or when one octave-band level penetrates into the contours at least 5 dB(A) more than does any other octave-band level. The true sound level will then be a little less than that indicated by the figure. The maximum possible error is 5 dB(A).

* This method is not included in National or International standards.

HML method

8   The HML (high, medium and low) method only requires measurement of the A-weighted (L_A) and C-weighted (L_C) sound pressure levels. The A-weighted and C-weighted sound pressure levels are used with three ear protector values H - high, M - medium and L - low.

9   The effective A-weighted sound pressure level at the ear, L'_A, is calculated in two steps:

Step 1   The predicted noise level reduction (PNR) is calculated from one of two formulae:

If L_C-L_A is less than or equal to 2:

$$PNR = M - \frac{(H\text{-}M)}{4} \times (L_C - L_A - 2)$$

If L_C-L_A is more than 2:

$$PNR = M - \frac{(M\text{-}L)}{8} \times (L_C - L_A - 2)$$

Step 2   The PNR is subtracted from the A-weighted noise level, L_A, to give L'_A.

10   A worked example of this method is given in Appendix 9.

SNR method

11   The SNR (single number rating) method only requires measurement of the C-weighted sound pressure levels.

12   The effective A-weighted sound pressure level at the ear, L'_A, is given by subtracting the SNR value from the C-weighted sound pressure level L_C. A worked example is given in Appendix 10.

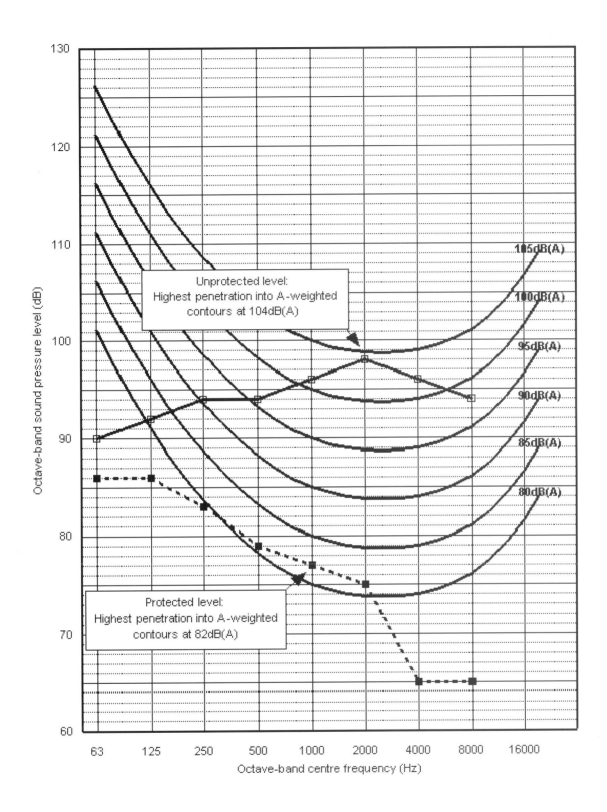

Figure A1 Example of graphical octave-band method. The octave-band levels from the example of Appendix 8 have been plotted, with and without the ear protector APVs applied. The graph shows both protected and unprotected spectra (ie the sound pressure level at the ear either without or with ear protectors fitted)

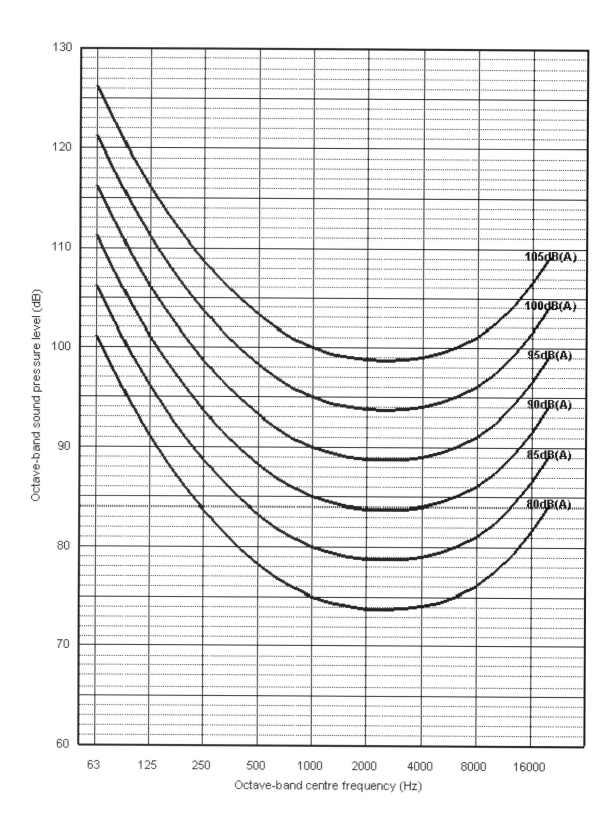

Figure A2 Blank form for graphical octave-band method

Appendix 8   Octave-band method worked example

The characteristics of the noise:

L_A (or L_{eq} in dB(A)) measured over one (or more) complete cycle: 103.2 dB(A)								
Noise spectrum, average value over one or more complete machine cycles:								
Octave-band centre frequency (Hz)	63	125	250	500	1000	2000	4000	8000
1 Unweighted SPL (dB)	90	92	94	94	96	98	96	94

The ear protector is supplied with the following octave-band information:

This ear protection comes with BS EN 24869-1 attenuation data supplied by the manufacturer:								
Octave-band centre frequency (Hz)	63	125	250	500	1000	2000	4000	8000
Mean attenuation (dB)	7.4	10.0	14.4	19.6	22.8	29.6	38.8	34.1
Std.dev. (dB)	3.3	3.6	3.6	4.6	4.0	6.2	7.4	5.2
2 Assumed protection value (APV) (dB)	4.1	6.4	10.8	15.0	18.8	23.4	31.4	28.9

The A-weighted sound pressure level at the ear can now be calculated using the APVs:

When ear protection is worn, the level at the ear in each octave-band is calculated by subtracting the APVs from the octave-band sound pressure levels (line 1 - line 2 = line 3):								
Octave-band centre frequency (Hz):	63	125	250	500	1000	2000	4000	8000
3 SPL - APV:	85.9	85.6	83.2	79.0	77.2	74.6	64.6	65.1
To calculate the effective A-weighted sound pressure level at the ear, L'_A, A-weighting factors need to be added to the protected sound pressure level at each frequency (line 3 + line 4 = line 5):								
4 A-weighting factors (AW):	-26.2	-16.1	-8.6	-3.2	0.0	1.2	1.0	-1.1
5 L'_A = (SPL - APV) + AW	59.7	69.5	74.6	75.8	77.2	75.8	65.6	64.0
These A-weighted levels must be summed. To do this the level must first be converted from decibels to a value related to energy: antilog (A-weighted SPL at the ear/10), which is equivalent to $10^{(L'A/10)}$ (line 5/10 = line 6).								
6 $L'_A/10$	5.97	6.95	7.46	7.58	7.72	7.58	6.56	6.40
antilog ($L'_A/10$):	933254	8912509	28840315	38018940	52480746	38018940	3630781	2511886
Now these values can be summed and the result converted back to an A-weighted sound pressure level using 10 x log (sum):								
Sum: 173 347 371								
A-weighted sound pressure level = 10 x $\log_{10}$(173 347 371): 82.4 dB(A)								
Round to the nearest whole number: **82 dB(A)**								

Appendix 9   HML method worked example

The characteristics of the noise from the machine are:

L_A (or A-weighted L_{eq}):	103.2 dB(A)
L_C (or C-weighted L_{eq}):	103.4 dB(C)

The ear protection comes with the following HML data:

H:	25 dB
M:	19 dB
L:	13 dB

The effective A-weighted sound pressure level at the ear can be estimated using the HML attenuation values.

The predicted noise level reduction (PNR) is calculated from the H, M and L factors. The formula used depends on the difference between L_C and L_A.	
If L_C - L_A is less than or equal to 2:	$PNR = M - \frac{(H-M)}{4} \times (L_C - L_A - 2)$
If L_C - L_A is greater than 2:	$PNR = M - \frac{(M-L)}{8} \times (L_C - L_A - 2)$

The A-weighted sound pressure level at the ear is given by subtracting the appropriate PNR value (rounded to the nearest whole number) from the measured A-weighted sound pressure level (L_A).

In this example L_C - L_A = 0.2 dB, therefore the first equation for PNR is used:

PNR = 19 - (25 - 19)/4 x (0.2 - 2)	21.7 dB
A-weighted sound pressure level at the ear = L_A - PNR	81.5 dB(A)
Round to the nearest whole number	**82 dB(A)**

Appendix 10   SNR method worked example

The characteristics of the noise from the machine are:

L_C (or C-weighted L_{eq}):	103.4 dB(C)

The ear protection comes with the following SNR data:

SNR	22 dB

The A-weighted sound pressure level at the ear can be estimated using the SNR value.

The effective A-weighted sound pressure level at the ear is given by subtracting the SNR value from the L_C (or C-weighted L_{eq}):	
A-weighted SPL at the ear = L_C - SNR =	81.4 dB(A)
Round to the nearest whole number	**81 dB(A)**

Appendix 11 Methods for predicting the reduction in peak SPL given by ear protection

1   For impulsive noises, such as power presses, forges or the firing of explosives or firearms, the main purpose is often to ensure that the effective peak sound pressure level at the ear is below the peak action level.

2   The normal methods of estimating the effectiveness of ear protectors are not suitable for predicting the peak sound pressure level reduction. A simple method, described in BS EN 458: 1994, has been shown to give acceptable results for mid- and high-frequency impulsive noise.

3   The method is applicable to most types of industrial impulsive noise, where the noise is not dominated by low-frequency components. The frequency content of the impulsive noise is assessed by determining the difference between the A-weighted and C-weighted maximum sound pressure levels measured using the fast ('F') time weighting on a sound level meter. If this value is less than 5 dB, then the predicted reduction in the peak sound pressure level is equal to the M-value (of the HML values, see Appendix 6). A worked example is given in Appendix 12.

4   This method is not applicable to impulsive noise which is predominantly low frequency. No recognised method is available (in 1997) for predicting the performance of ear protectors in this type of noise. Specialised measurements have to be made of the actual sound pressure level under the protector.

Appendix 12   Worked example of the selection of ear protection for impulsive noise

The characteristics of the noise are:

Peak, C-weighted, sound pressure level	147.8 dB(C)
Maximum value of the A and C weighted SPLs using the 'F' (fast) response of the sound level meter:	
$L_{A,fast,max}$	125.4 dB(A)
$L_{C,fast,max}$	128.7 dB(C)

The ear protection comes with the following HML data:

H:	25 dB
M:	19 dB
L:	13 dB

Whether this method may be used or not, depends on the difference between the two parameters $L_{C,fast,max}$ and $L_{A,fast,max}$:

If $L_{C,fast,max}$ - $L_{A,fast,max}$ is less than 5 dB:	The M-value can be used as the predicted noise level reduction (PNR).
If $L_{C,fast,max}$ - $L_{A,fast,max}$ is 5 or more:	Low frequencies dominate the noise. The sound pressure level at the ear can only be determined by direct measurement.

In this example $L_{C,fast,max}$ - $L_{A,fast,max}$ = 3.3 dB, therefore the M value may be used.

The estimated effective peak sound pressure level at the ear is calculated by subtracting the M-value from the peak SPL:

effective peak SPL = 147.8 - 19 =	**128.8 dB(C)**

References

1   *The Act outlined* HSC2 HSE Books 1975

2   *Management of health and safety at work. Management of Health and Safety at Work Regulations 1992. Approved Code of Practice* L21 HSE Books 1992 ISBN 0 7176 0412 8

3   *Health surveillance in noisy industries: Advice for employers* INDG193 HSE Books 1995 (Available free for single copies or in priced packs on ISBN 0 7176 0933 2)

4   *New and expectant mothers at work: A guide for employers* HSG122 HSE Books 1994 ISBN 0 7176 0826 3

5   *Young people at work: A guide for employers* HSG165 HSE Books 1997 ISBN 0 7176 1285 6

6   *Sound solutions: Techniques to reduce noise at work* HSG138 HSE Books 1995 ISBN 0 7176 0791 7

7   *Keep the noise down: Advice for purchasers of workplace machinery* INDG263 HSE Books 1997. Available free for single copies or in priced packs on ISBN 0 7176 1480 8

8   *The Health and Safety Executive: Working with employers* HSE35 HSE Books 1996

9   *Machinery: Guidance notes on UK Regulations* URN 95/650 DTI 1995

10   BS EN ISO 12001: 1997 *Acoustics - Noise emitted by machinery and equipment - Rules for the drafting and presentation of a noise test code*

11   *Safety signs and signals. Guidance on Regulations. The Health and Safety (Safety Signs and Signals) Regulations 1996* L64 HSE Books 1996 ISBN 0 7176 0870 0

12   *Selecting a health and safety consultancy* INDG133 HSE Books 1994

Further reading

Priced publications

A guide to audiometric testing programmes Guidance Note MS 26 HSE Books 1995 ISBN 0 7176 0942 1

Control of noise in quarries HSG109 HSE Books 1993 ISBN 0 7176 0648 1

Hearing protection: An interactive learning programme (A multi-media CD-ROM training package to instruct the wearers of hearing protection) HSE Books 1996 ISBN 0 7176 1210 4

Noise control in the rubber industry HSE Books 1990 ISBN 0 11 885550 6

Noise from pneumatic systems Guidance Note PM 56 HSE Books 1985 ISBN 0 11 883529 7

Noise reduction at buckle folding machines HSE Books 1986 ISBN 0 11 883849 0

Noise reduction at web-fed presses HSE Books 1988 ISBN 0 11 883972 1

Protection of hearing in the paper and board industry HSE Books 1988 ISBN 0 11 883971 3

Safety representatives and safety committees L87 HSE Books 1996 ISBN 0 7176 1220 1

The costs and benefits of the Noise at Work Regulations 1989 Contract Research Report CRR116 HSE Books 1996 ISBN 0 7176 1266 X

Free leaflets

Ear protection in noisy firms: Employers' duties explained INDG200 HSE Books 1995

Hear this (a pocket card for workers on ear protection) INDG201P HSE Books 1995

Introducing the Noise at Work Regulations: A brief guide to the requirements controlling noise at work INDG75(rev) HSE Books 1989

Noise (Agriculture Series) AS8(rev) HSE Books 1989

Noise at work: A guide for employees INDG99(rev1) HSE Books 1997

Noise in construction: Further guidance on the Noise at Work Regulations 1989 INDG127(rev) HSE Books 1994

Woodworking Information Sheets - WIS4 *Noise reduction at band re-saws* HSE Books 1992, WIS5 *Noise enclosure at band re-saws* HSE Books 1992, WIS8 *Noise reduction at multi-spindle planing and moulding machines* HSE Books 1992 and WIS13 *Noise at woodworking machines* HSE Books 1994

Note: Many HSE leaflets are available free for single copies, but multiple orders may be supplied in priced packs.

The future availability and accuracy of the references listed in this publication cannot be guaranteed.

For details of how to obtain HSE priced and free publications, see back cover.

British Standards are available from BSI Sales and Customer Services, 389 Chiswick High Road, London W4 4AL Tel: 0181 996 7000 Fax: 0181 996 7001.

The Stationery Office (formerly HMSO) publications are available from The Publications Centre, PO Box 276, London SW8 5DT.
Tel: 0171 873 9090. They are also available from bookshops.

Glossary

A-weighting　A weighting of the audible frequencies designed to reflect the response of the human ear to noise. The ear is more sensitive to noise at frequencies in the middle of the audible range than it is to either very high or very low frequencies. Noise measurements are often A-weighted (using a dedicated filter) to compensate for the sensitivity of the ear.

Absorption　The ability of a material to soak up noise energy converting it into heat (reduction of sound energy using sound absorbing materials, eg mineral wool).

Active noise control (ANR)　The reduction or cancellation of one sound by the introduction of a second sound having equal amplitude, but with a reversed phase (see *Sound solutions*).

Airborne noise　Noise transmitted through the air.

Assumed protection value (APV)　Manufacturers supply average attenuation values for hearing protection, along with standard deviation figures (indications of the accuracy of the averages). To predict the noise reduction which might be achieved in real use, an assumed protection value is used, usually taken to be the mean attenuation minus one standard deviation.

Attenuation　Noise reduction, measured in decibels.

Audiometry　A method of assessing the degree of hearing loss of a person.

C-weighting　A weighting of the audible frequencies often used for measurement of peak sound pressure level. The A-weighting is not appropriate at very high noise levels; as the noise level increases the ear is better able to hear low and high frequency. C-weighting has an almost flat (or linear) response across the audible frequency range. (Note: for normal measurements of peak noise, C-weighting should be used, but if the peak noise contains a large proportion of low- or high-frequency sound, then the use of C-weighting may give erroneous results).

Calibration　A check of the function of a sound level meter by comparing the meter reading with a known sound pressure level.

CE marking　A label used to show that a machine or an ear protector conforms to the specification of a European Directive.

Competent person　A person with sufficient knowledge and experience to undertake a noise assessment. A competent person will not need an advanced knowledge of acoustics, but will be able to work unsupervised, will need a good understanding and practical experience of what information needs to be obtained, how to use and look after the instruments involved, and how to present the information in an intelligible manner (see Parts 3 and 4).

Cycle (machine cycle)　An operation or sequence of operations (of a machine) which is repeated.

Constrained layer　A combination of materials, one of which is a damping element.

Daily personal noise exposure ($L_{EP,d}$)　A measure of the average noise energy a person is exposed to during a working day. The $L_{EP,d}$ is directly related to the risk of hearing damage.

Damping　Control measure to deaden the tendency of machine parts to 'ring'.

Decibel (dB)　The units of sound level and noise exposure measurement.

dB(A)　Decibels A-weighted

dB(C)　Decibels C-weighted

Dosemeter	Instrument designed to continuously measure noise exposure. Usually worn on the person during their normal daily work operations. Useful for measuring a highly mobile person's noise exposure.	**Hearing protection**	See ear protection.
Earmuff	Ear protection consisting of a cup enclosing the outer ear.	**HML method**	A method of estimating the attenuation of hearing protection based on three parameters provided by the hearing protection manufacturer: H-High, M-Medium, L-Low.
Earplug	Ear protection in the form of a plug which is inserted into the entrance to the ear canal.	**Hz**	Hertz, the unit of frequency.
Ear protection	A term used to cover all forms of ear protection. It has the same meaning when used as 'hearing protection'.	**Integrating sound level meter**	A sound level meter which can accumulate the total sound energy over a specified period and computes an average (in dB(A)). Used for measuring a fluctuating sound level.
Ear protection zone	An area where a person is likely to be exposed to the second action level or above or to the peak action level or above, which has to be demarcated with a suitable sign to conform with regulation 9(1).	**Impulsive noise**	Any type of single or repeated noise of short duration, eg the noise from an explosion or the noise of a power press.
Enclosure	Noise control where the noise source is covered by a specially designed 'acoustic box' which stops the airborne noise reaching a receiver.	**Insulation**	A material which reduces sound passing through its thickness.
Equivalent continuous sound pressure level (L_{eq})	A measure of the average sound pressure level during a period of time, in dB.	**Isolation**	A means of controlling the noise path through a structure by interrupting that path.
		L_A	A-weighted L_{eq} in dB(A).
Fluid-borne noise	Noise transmitted through a fluid, such as a hydraulic system.	L_C	C-weighted L_{eq} in dB(C).
Fractional noise exposure	Personal exposure related to part of the working day or an activity.	$L_{A,fast\ max.}$	Maximum value of the A-weighted sound pressure level, measured using the fast (F) time weighting (in dB(A)).
Frequency (Hz)	The pitch of the sound, measured in Hertz.	$L_{C,fast\ max.}$	Maximum value of the C-weighted sound pressure level, measured using fast (F) time weighting (in dB(C)).
Frequency analysis	Analysis of a sound into its frequency components.	L_{eq}	See 'Equivalent continuous sound pressure level'.
Hazard	Anything that has the potential to cause harm. Noise can cause harm to hearing.	$L_{EP,d}$	See 'Daily personal noise exposure'.
		$L_{EP,w}$	Weekly personal noise exposure.
		L_{EX}	Also used as a term for $L_{EP,d}$.

Level-dependent (or amplitude-sensitive) earmuffs	Earmuffs designed to protect against hazardous noise while permitting good communication during quiet periods.	**Pa**	Pascal, unit of measurement of sound pressure.
Narrow band noise	Division of the frequency content of a noise into bands of fixed width (eg 1 Hz band width).	**Pa²-hours (Pa².h)**	The units of noise exposure for measurements made using a dosemeter.
Neighbourhood noise	Noise which affects the environment and people's everyday life.	**Passive level-dependent earmuffs**	Ear protection muffs (non-electronic) with an acoustic filter which allows the transmission of low sound pressures with little attenuation, but gives greater attenuation at high sound pressures.
Noise assessment	The determination of the noise exposure of a person or group of people.	**Peak sound pressure level**	The maximum value reached by the sound pressure at any instant during a measurement period (in dB, usually with either C or linear frequency weighting).
Noise emission	The measured sound emitted by a noise source.		
Noise exposure	A measure of the total sound energy a person is exposed to. It is dependent on both the sound pressure level to which the person is exposed and the time over which the exposure occurs.	**Permanent threshold shift (PTS)**	Permanent deafness after prolonged exposure to high sound levels. An irreversible process.
		Personal sound exposure meter	See 'Dosemeter'.
Noise spectrum	A noise represented by its frequency components.	**Predicted noise level reduction (PNR)**	The noise reduction predicted using manufacturers' attenuation data.
Noise survey	A survey of noise levels at specified locations in a work area before making a full noise assessment.	**Reverberation**	The sound from a noise source being reflected from walls, floors, ceilings and obstacles within a room before being absorbed. If many reflections occur before absorption, the reflected noise adds to that directly from the noise source, increasing the overall sound level.
Noise refuge	An operator enclosure in which a person can work away from the source of noise.		
Nuisance noise	Noise which is usually not damaging but is a cause of annoyance.	**Risk**	The chance that someone will be harmed by a hazard.
Octave-bands	A division of the frequency range into bands, the upper frequency limit of each band being twice the lower frequency limit. The width of the octave-bands increases at higher frequencies.	**Semi-insert ear protectors**	Ear protection in the form of an ear-canal cap, which is held against the entrance to the ear canal by a headband.
1/3 Octave-band	Single octave-bands divided into three parts.	**Sound exposure level (SEL, SEL$_A$, SEL$_C$)**	A measure of the sound energy in a short duration event, such as an explosion. The SEL is defined as: 'The sound pressure level (in dB) which, if it lasted for 1 second, would produce the same energy as the actual noise event'.
Octave-band centre frequency	The frequency at the centre of an octave-band.		

Sound intensity A measure of the flow of sound energy.

Sound level meter (SLM) Instrument for measuring various noise parameters.

Sound power level A measure of the total acoustic power produced by a noise source.

Sound pressure level (SPL) The basic measure of noise loudness, expressed in decibels, usually measured with an appropriate frequency weighting (eg the A-weighted SPL in dB(A)).

Sound restoration level-dependent earmuffs Earmuffs incorporating an electronic sound reproduction system. At low levels of noise the sound detected by a microphone on the outside of the muff is relayed to a loudspeaker in the muff cup. At higher levels of noise the electronics cut out the reproduced sound, leaving the inherent attenuation of the earmuff to provide the protection.

Single number rating (SNR) A method of estimating the attenuation of ear protection based on a single parameter given by the ear protection manufacturer.

Temporary threshold shift (TTS) Temporary sensation of deafness after high noise exposure which recovers with time.

Tinnitus Involuntary noises in the ear such as 'ringing', often associated with hearing loss.

Transmission The ability of noise to travel through something with an attenuation in the noise level.

Verification Periodic tests for sound level meters to ensure that they conform to standard specifications.

Workstation The position of an operator where noise levels are measured.

WITHDRAWN

Printed and published by the Health and Safety Executive   4/98   C120

92